Indian IT Saga

About the Author

Dr. Utpal K. Banerjee took his honour's degree in Pure Physics (1955) from the University of Calcutta with a graduate Scholarship and his Ph.D from the University of Manchester, U.K. (1972) where he was awarded a Commonwealth scholarship for doctoral research.

His vast experience in matters relating to information management and allied subjects stems from his close association with the Ministries of Defence, Finance, Industry and the Directorate General of Technical Development where he served in senior official capacities for 17 years. After resigning from Government service, he worked with Tata Steel as their Chief of Mangement Services, with the Administrative Staff College of India as Director of Computer Division and with computronics India as Senior Executive Director. He took over as Director General of All India Management Association for 5 years, to run the national apex body for promoting Indian and international management, ushering in computerization bringing UNESCO support and arranging global "teleconference". Since 1990, he is a highly successful adviser and consultant in information technmology with several large public and private bodies.

Indian IT Saga

Growth to Glory

Utpal K. Banerjee

Jointly published for

ICEIT
ICT inspired

Institution of Communication Engineers
and Information Technologists
and

NET*Comm Labs*
Netcomm Labs Pvt. Ltd.
by

CONCEPT PUBLISHING COMPANY PVT. LTD.,
NEW DELHI-110059

ISBN-13 : 978-93-5125-061-6

First Published 2014

Published and Printed by

Concept Since 1974

Concept Publishing Company Pvt. Ltd.
A/15-16, Commercial Block, Mohan Garden
New Delhi-110059 (India)
T: 25351460, 25351794, *F*: 091-11-25357109
E: publishing@conceptpub.com, W: www.conceptpub.com
Editorial Office: H-13, Bali Nagar, New Delhi-110 015, India.

Cataloging in Publication Data—*Courtesy:* D.K. Agencies (P) Ltd. <docinfo@dkagencies.com>

Banerjee, Utpal K. (Utpal Kumar), 1935-
Indian IT saga : growth to glory / Utpal K. Banerjee.
p. cm.
Includes bibliographical references (p.) and index.
ISBN 9789351250616

1. Information technology—India—History. I. Title. II. Title: Indian information technology saga.

DDC 303.48330954 23

Dedicated

To

Brig. S.V.S. Chowdhry (Retd.),

Former President of 'CSI' and 'IETE',

And

A Life-Long Companion,

For

Persuading Me to Write This Book

And Providing Myriad Suggestions,

And

Prof. H.M. Gupta,

Of IIT, Delhi and President, 'ICEIT',

For

'ICEIT' Sponsoring Publication of This Book

Preface

Information Revolution arrived in India almost stealthily, — through small, hesitant steps. This was four decades ago when there was a lot of initial hesitation, as the incipient technology was least understood by common man. The machine (hardware) — once given instructions (software) by its human masters — would work incredibly fast, with extraordinary accuracy and produce almost instantaneous results, but it was instantly feared by many to be a 'labour killing' device. It was seen to be snatching away manual jobs, — almost in the same way as the Luddites viewed, during the early Industrial Revolution in the West, the steam engines to be snatching away hundreds of jobs from coachmen and cabby drivers, making the horse-driven buggies redundant. In the 60's, the apprehension in India led to unrest among thousands of bank employees, for whom two successive committees under Dr. Rangarajan (later the Reservc Bank Governor) had to lay down specific criteria under which ledgers and manual folios would be printed by machines, only to a limited extent. In the life insurance sector, the attempt to issue premium notices from the machine, based on policy records, created considerable misapprehension, and even threats of strike, among the large number of insurance employees. In the 70's, ASCI, Hyderabad Court of Governors — where current and former chairmen of Hindustan Lever, STC, Punjab National Bank and other large corporations were present — decided against recommending computors to Indian organisations: almost on the grounds of man *versus* machine ! As late as the 90's, the introduction in Tata Steel of enterprise resource planning — using comprehensive, bundled software — was expected to increase efficiency manifold and reduce business inefficiency. But even this was resisted by the workers, fearing redundancy, even in the venerable organisation known for its half- century of record of no labour unrest !

Hardware and software — combined with national and international communication facility — is today part of information technology (IT). IT has ushered in an Information Revolution is because it has, for the first time in human history, dared to increase brain power of common man, — going much beyond its predecessor Industrial Revolution where steam, electricity and gasoline had enhanced man's muscle power manifold. IT essentially adds to human intelligence: by providing speed, accuracy, reliability and capacity to solve problems and taking decisions, — while all the time remaining as a tool, ever amenable to be applied in myriad different ways. How this has happened — and is still happening in an accelerated tempo — in India and bringing in a cultural change makes for a fascinating story. The dynamic changes in popular culture, that have become perceptible and near palpable, can be unspooled: frame-by-frame: over broad decades.

× × ×

The second generation of IT (soon after the first generation of unwieldy valves) had just about learnt to work with 0 and 1 on its transistors in the mid-fifties. Instead of the inconvenient way of stringing numbers and carrying zillions of calculations needed by accountants, the machine could store astronomical sums and carry out most difficult computations in a trice. This happened in India in the 60's and all accounts people embraced the technology, not because they understood it, but because payrolls could be rolled out faster, materials could be accounted for, sales ledgers could be maintained accurately and produced in time, accounts journals and documents could lead to timely closure and, at the year-end, lead to trial balances and balance sheets in time. So, all routine record-keeping activities got transferred to machines: in TISCO, TELCO, Indian Railways, BHEL, HAL and scores of other big and small organisations in the country, and IT was placed under the finance heads, as they used it most.

This was the 'data processing' age, when massive input data would be taken to computers and large chunks of outputs taken out for distribution and analysis. Gradually, larger benefits started seeping in and are still happening around. Bank after nationalised and private bank began inter-branch reconciliation: for all the outstanding debits and credits. Now, the unreconciled vouchers represented money kept out of the banking systems, and in several cases, actually led to serious frauds and scams, involving crores of rupees. Inter-branch and, later, inter-bank reconciliations among vouchers — followed by drafts, credit cards, traveller cheques — brought in more accounted-for money in the Indian banks and led to their increased activities, opening of more branches and, eventually, more employment for bank clerks, A spin-off activity was computer-based monitoring of loans and advances: given to a very large segment of small-time borrowers under the 'social banking' schemes. A better progress chasing and redress in time made for improved loan recovery and reduced incidence of doubtful debts (and even 'bad' debts). This experience is from SBI and covers Bihar, among others — making again for better banking health and more branches with increased manpower deployment. Simultaneously, this led to borrowers achieving speedy payment of interest and capital, and doing better small-time business. This applies all the way for NABARD and various large and medium cooperatives. For the life insurance, assigning routine premium notice and recovery business to computers left more time to the supervisors to do only trouble-shooting and, for the managers, to devise newer schemes of insurance, — thus increasing business volume and providing more employment. So, the 'revolution' was happening at last in 'labour enhancement' "!

One area, helping to change popular culture in the 'data processing' times of the 60's and 70's, belonged to State secondary and higher secondary boards. The number of examinees for any State would run usually into several lakhs and using computers even as 'glorified type-writers' — for receiving coded answer-papers, decoding and totalling them, preparing mark-sheets, and issuing gazette notifications — all led to substantial confidentiality, accurate mark-sheets, speedy announcement of results and, on the whole, vastly increased student satisfaction and parental relief from anxiety: for delayed, inaccurate or leaked results. The second area pertained to electricity billing for State electricity boards. Again, meter-readings (when available, average otherwise) were fed to computer centres to prepare bills and issue them to consumers for recovery. In the western UP alone, this increased revenue by several crores and, at the same time, reduced corruption in non-preparation and non-issue of bills during the earlier manual system.

The Indian States have their AGs who used 'data processing' to build their revenue systems from chalans and related documents. Some innovative States like Karnataka concentrated on the differences between revenue recoverable and that recovered, commodity-wise, location-wise, establishment-wise and area-wise: to institute mechanisms like special inspectors, 'flying squads', etc., for speedier recovery or penal action. For Indian industry, such revenue-increasing activities by using 'data processing' were many and varied. Planning blast furnace 're-lining' for speedy maintenance, blending of coal from different mining sources, 'bills of material' for engineering jobs, creation of pension funds for timely disbursement, wage-board negotiations were some of the areas affecting directly or indirectly managerial and popular perception of IT. In some cases, mathematical analysis and statistical forecasting were dovetailed on accumulated data for production planning in factories, budget forecasting for banks and demand-supply matching for hospital medicines. Such applications vastly improved managerial decision-making in public and private domains, — for reducing costs, increasing profit or revenue, saving time and improving overall productivity and efficiency.

× × ×

By the 70's, the third-generation IT (with integrated circuits) was able to process a single input and to provide the result pretty fast, before picking up the next input. This development was a quantum jump, in ushering in the 'on-line transaction processing' era, with the help of medium and mini-computers. Indian Railways reaped the best benefit by providing passenger reservation, — by any train, for any destination, on any date, in any class, honouring any quota and for any return journey. The common traveller was an immense gainer: increasing convenience and substantially cutting out graft. Even the booking clerks gained: by eliminating tedious day-end cash reconciliation. Newer trains could be introduced easily without increasing the booking-office overload. Remote terminals to the local computer-clusters were used to collect the return information.

'On-line transaction processing' was an immense boon to the industrial and changed the management culture overnight. Steel making in all the Indian steel plants got a boost by introducing mini-computers to pick-up sample-data on hot iron and accordingly released oxygen at desired pressure, temperature and volume: neither too early nor too late; neither too much nor too little; neither too fast nor too slow. Such accuracy cut out bad-quality steel drastically and increased profitability sky-high, virtually making the plants turn round. On-line sheering machines cut billets to eliminate end-rejections and shaped plates from the hot plate mills in the requisite sizes to reduce wastage. The principle applied down the line to other on-line controls in industrial applications and improved immensely their productivity and profit.

The Information Revolution was catching up with India very fast and, by the early 80's, came in the personal computers (PCs), on single microchips, that brought in another sea change in the scene. Adopted on individual desks, a PC was a complete computer and immediately released several personal and office productivity tools. Secretaries and personal assistants, copywriters and journalists, teachers and researchers, doctors and lawyers — literally everybody — jumped on the bandwagon of 'word processing' and threw away their antiquated typewriters in favour of neat writing and a zillion provisions for additions and deletions, font-selections, margin adjustments, drastic alterations, cutting and pasting, and so on and so forth. Presentations could be worked out by promoters and advertisers; office management streamlined through help from software by managers; and pages composed and laid out by editors and publishers. Personalised calculation tables and their umpteen revisions through electronic spreadsheets were available to project-planners: neatly arranged databases, with relationships well defined, virtually for anybody who cared for a systematic databank, — starting with a telephone directory onwards. All these facilities continue to grow and multiply by the day, with novel offer of useful databases on sale all the time.

If 'word processing' comes, can 'image processing' be far behind? Indeed, engineers and draftsmen showed the way with computer-aided design (CAD) and drafting software. Every engineering organisation from EIL to RITES, from BHEL to HAL and HEC, every engineering college faculty and student, every technician has obtained an order-of-magnitude jump in his or her convenience by its use: for learning, designing and planning, and for any construction and execution of an engineering project. Another exciting area of 'image processing' is its limitless use with the remote sensing satellites of India that are hovering overhead at 700-900 km and sending endless data on our natural resources like glacial waters, forests, crops, overground waters, landmasses, soil, underground waters, minerals, fish and sea-bed mineral. They use both spectral data and infrared radiation data, — needing digital analysis and image processing, before their knowledge can be harnessed into planning and improving the common man's lot. A few examples could be to analyse satellite pictures over space and time, in order to: anticipate drought or floods for the snow-fed rivers for untimely or altered glacial melting; taking timely steps against wide-spread crop-diseases; look for forest-cutting and go for afforestation; alter cropping patterns, where needed; discover new 'aquifers' for solving drinking water problems; dig new mines in prospective areas, reclaim wetland; and explore ocean beds for mineral extraction. A concrete instance has been knowing from satellite imagery how the highly-prized tuna fish came to the shallow waters in the afternoon hours and setting up fishermen's coops and trawler facilities in the coastal districts to increase their livelihood by several orders. Geo-stationary satellites, at 36,000 km each, have hugely added to the telecom facilities. India is among a handful of countries who have such launching facilities and is a major FE earner.

× × ×

By the 80's, another vista opened up: with computers connecting to each other and forming networks. With local, metropolitan and national networks, computers began sharing their resources among nearby buildings, all over the cities and the entire country. In the meantime, computing power was growing and there appeared on the scene mainframe (i.e., large) and even super computers. Now all these computers could hold hands with each other, figuratively speaking and introduce enormous flexibility in their modes of connections, — with a vastly increased potential for new usages for common man. To take an example, India Meteorology Department installed a supercomputer, which could now do highly complicated calculations for medium-term (say, over 48-72 hours) weather forecasting, in place of the earlier short-term forecasting for only 24 hours. This meant power to forecast storms and cyclones and broadcast over the high seas, 2 3 days in advance, so that the fishermen — who sail out far away for their catch for days together — could return to the safety of hearth and home, in time. For all the coastal States, this was a matter of life and death for the fisher folk where IT came to their rescue. Another example is ONGC's mini-super computer at Dehra Dun —

networked with other computers in Mumbai, Kolkata and Vadodra — in order to process seismic information from the on-shore teams and offshore ships that keep collecting data from under earth (or under seabed) on likely occurrence of oil and natural gas. For a country that gets the bulk of its petroleum resources from abroad at high cost, this is a vital area of concern to the national economy.

The Indian Airlines (and later the private airlines, when they were born), Air India and eventually the travel agents have caught on with passenger reservation and cargo-handling facilities on line, on a nation-wide basis. They are connected to SITA, the global network of airlines computers, to provide the same facilities anywhere, anytime. Organisations and industries like RBI and SBI (also connected to the global banking computer network SWIFT), SAIL, Tata Steel, BHEL, NTPC, Coal India, NSE and BSE, PTI, Oil India and a host of other bodies are forming their own computer networks: bringing in a huge change in their work culture and reaping enormous benefits that ultimately trickle down to the masses. Indian Railways, for instance, is using a mini-super computer for developing on-line Freight Operation and Information System: to closely monitor the goods traffic through wagons all over the country, so that speedier operations can be achieved over our vast land. Indian Police is working on crime-criminal information (with past records, modes of operation, territorial distribution and personal description) to have speedier apprehensions and convictions, and better the common man's lot.

Most comprehensive IT activity was nucleated by National Informatics Centre (NIC), beginning from late 70's,—at national, State, union territory, district and block levels. IT support has been planned and implemented for information analysis, appropriate studies, design and development of applications, and necessary training and education. NIC's major achievements include: District Information System for economic and social development, programme implementation and project monitoring in every district, General Information Service terminals on a country-wide basis for providing data on national economy, infrastructure, service activities and IMF and World Bank; Medical Information System to furnish network access for global knowledge to specialists and physicians; and industry-information linkages. Court Information System, in particular, helps Supreme Court and its litigants with daily 'list of business', automatic distribution of fresh cases (thus eliminating corruption) and caveat-matching, — linked to 18 High Courts in the country as a gateway on case-status and daily case-lists.

A notable venture, beginning in the 80's, was computerised rural information system project (CRISP) on a totally decentralised basis: starting from Karnataka's Karwar district and extended elsewhere. These activities have now been subsumed in the NIC's functions. Pilot projects on land-records computerisation (providing *patta* to the farmers, with copies to others, to eliminate coercion and corruption) were first tried out in ten districts and have now been extended to cover gradually over thc entire country

× × ×

In the 90's, India, and the world, was witness to a new phenomenon: the Internet, as a network of computer networks, making use of global communication facilities. The Internet service-providers set afoot a highly flexible World-Wide Web, where data and information could be sent to anybody, anywhere, at the cost of a local call. Limited organisational versions of the Internet, called 'Intranet', also came in vogue. Taking advantage of the easy connectivity, many States have introduced 'e-governance' with focus on the masses, as illustrated below:

- AP — establishing 'information kiosks' for citizens paying taxes, collecting birth/death certificates, SC/ST certificates and land-registration deeds;
- Kerala — intending to make it an 'intelligent state' with 100% literacy, reducing unemployment and ensuring administration to be citizen-friendly;
- MP — attempting social engineering through *Soochanalaya* (information centre) on low-cost commercial lines, through an Intranet for *Gyandoot* (purveyor of knowledge): to cover development needs of government departments and Panchayats in all blocks of Dhar district.

Examination results of CBSE and other boards are now posted, thanks to the efforts of NIC, on the Internet, maintaining full confidentiality under individual roll-numbers. This interestingly has a social dimension where the student does not have to face the glare of attention from others in front of a public notice board and suicide cases would come down. Another application is the publicising of agricultural prices for *mandis*. Out of 7,000 *mandis* in India, 800 *mandis* have information on agricultural commodities (including vegetables and other perishable products) put on the Internet and made available to farmers at 'Internet Kiosks' using simple PCs. Later, NIC proposes to make them SMS-enabled

This marks IT's transition to the 00's, which is the age of mobile phones. The latter is a very strong IT-device, numbering already some 20-30 million in India and set very soon to outpace the landlines. It already provides many facilities of the desktop PCs, like e-mail and for farm-price publicity, Rs. 25,000 for a PC are way above Rs.300 for a mobile — with the technology capable of benefiting the common man, as far as delivery mechanism is concerned. Another application of the current decade is the Community Information Centre for remote places. All the 487 blocks of the North-East India, covering its eight States, have today 'Internet Kiosks', with satellite connectivity, 6 PCs and TV — to provide IT-based services like *mandi* prices, 'e-governance' (including certificates on birth, death, caste, income, etc.) and land records. Considering the time oft 10 days for a letter to reach North-East, a time of 10 minutes for an e-mail is no mean achievement, in reducing the distance-perception !

Using the Internet and powerful computer facilities, NIC's 'Citizen Services Gateways' have widely opened their portals. Whether it is a ration card in HP or on-line property valuation in Tamil Nadu or computerised telephone directories in MTNL in Mumbai and Delhi or downloading pension forms in MP, the list is already endless. A small illustrative sample is provided below:

- On-line Ticket Booking at Indian Airlines.
- List of Identified Jobs for Persons with Disabilities.
- Daily Orders and Cause List from District Courts of Delhi.
- Online Employment Status from Government of Tamil Nadu.
- Online Licenses and Permits in Andhra Pradesh.
- Online Status Enquiry for Passport.
- Book a Railway Ticket through the Net.
- Application Forms for getting a Driving License in Delhi.
- Acts and Rules from Ministry of Information and Broadcasting.
- Latest News from CBSE.
- Schemes from Sports Authority of India.
- Online Citizen Services from Himachal Pradesh Government.
- Citizen Charter of the Ministry of Coal.

- Model Code of Conduct from Election Commission of India.
- Missing Persons List from CBI.
- Online Status of Supreme Court Cases.
- Indian Airlines Flight Schedule.
- Online Application forms from Rural Electrification Corporation Ltd.
- Citizen Charter of the Ministry of Shipping.
- Get your new vehicle registered Online in Delhi.
- Modernisation Scheme for Central Government Organisations.
- Tourist Information from Jammu & Kashmir.
- Schemes for Rural Development in Assam.
- Travel Offers from Indian Airlines.
- Online Market Prices from National Horticulture Board.
- Recruitment Information from UPSC.
- Central Government Health Schemes.
- Online Application Forms from Department of Atomic Energy.
- Programmes and Schemes for Rural Development.
- Cause Lists of Indian Courts.
- Get a Digital Certificate from DGFT.
- Lodge your grievance with Delhi Minorities Commission.
- Strategies and Policies on AIDS Prevention.
- Research Activities of National Tuberculosis Institute.
- Data Base of HAJ Pilgrims.
- Auction of Air Tickets by Indian Airlines.
- Research in Homoeopathy.
- 'Wanted Persons' List from CBI.
- Pradhan Mantri Gram Sadak Yojana (PMGSY).
- Daily Orders of the Indian Courts.
- Investor Information from Coal India Ltd.
- Quality Certification for Agricultural Products (APEDA).
- Online Publications from Department of Education.
- Personal Banking from State Bank of India.
- Welfare Schemes for Tribals.
- Online Prices for Agricultural Commodities.
- Citizen Services of Gujarat Government.
- Check your IEC Status Online (Customs).
- Civil Services (Main) Examination Result.
- National Vocational Training Information Service.

- Holiday Ideas for Tourists.
- Parliament Bills and Acts Online.
- Weekly Wholesale Prices of Food Commodities (NAFED).
- Download Application forms of IDBI Services.
- Examination-Related Announcements by CBSE.
- Empanelment of Chartered Accountants at CAG.
- Daily Cause List of the Supreme Court.
- Database Services of Ministry of Labour.
- Formats of Affidavits required for a Passport.
- 'Companion Travel Offer' from Air India.
- PNR Status Online (Indian Railways).
- Foreign Currency Reference Rates (RBI).
- Agricultural Marketing Information Network.
- NCERT Books Online.
- Online Announcements from UPSC.
- Route Map for Delhi Metro Rail Service.
- Pravasi Bharatiya Divas for Indian Diaspora.
- Electronic Data Info Filing and Retrieval System (SEBI).
- Training Courses at Indian Space Research Organisation (ISRO).
- Travel Offers from Air India.
- Know About Service Taxes in India.
- Child Development Schemes.
- Online Application Forms from Directorate General Civil Aviation I.
- Forms for export of Horticulture Products from North-East.
- Obtain a certificate for physical handicap in Delhi.
- Cause List of Indian Courts.
- Indian Airlines Travel Offers.
- Multimedia Interactive Study Material for Schools.
- Income Tax Forms.
- Online Registration of Public Grievances.
- ICAR Guidelines for filing Patent Applications.
- Online Judgment Information System.
- Government Accommodation allotment waiting list.
- Online Forms from Employees Provident Fund Organisation.
- Email Facility for Indian Learning and Teaching Community.
- Guidelines for Foreigners Visiting Delhi.
- UPSC Examination Information.
- Get a Handicap Certificate in Delhi.

- Daily Orders of Supreme Court and High Courts.
- Information about UPSC Examinations.
- New Schemes of Central Government Housing Welfare Organization.
- Agricultural Marketing Information Network.
- Indian Railway's Train Schedule.
- Multimedia Interactive Study Material (School).
- Access Parliament Codes Online.
- Forms for filing Income Tax Returns Online Judgment Information System.
- Agricultural Marketing Information Network.
- Get a Voter's I Card in Delhi.
- Agricultural Marketing Information Network.
- Lodge a complaint with Central Vigilance Commission.
- Case Status of Supreme Court of India.
- Central Government Employees Housing Schemes.
- Income Tax Forms.
- 'Desh Videsh' Offer from Indian Airlines Write to the Prime Minister.
- Submit Opinion on Review of Working of Constitution.
- Stolen Vehicles Status (Delhi Police).
- File a Human Rights Violation Complaint.
- Access Parliament Acts Online.
- Check out your IEC Status at Custom (BIN).
- Form for opening a Post Office Savings Bank Account.
- Obtain an Excise Control Code (ECC) Number.
- Announcements for Overseas Study Scholarships.
- Application Form for PM's Rozgaar Yojana.
- Online Reservation Status at Indian Airlines.
- Indian Railways Train Schedule.
- Passport Forms.
- Stolen Vehicles Status (Delhi Police).

× × ×

In fine, IT has now arrived to the common man. The benefits of computerised voice mails for telephones, railways and airlines are at one's doorsteps and taken almost for granted. Media Lab Asia, launched at the government initiative since 2001, is now part of the Indian body politic: to work with industry, NGOs, government departments and public systems to bring IT innovations to every village. A few core projects have been:

- *Chikan-CAD Project* — For developing technologies and products, at IIT, Kanpur, for handicrafts, especially in Chikan embroidery.
- *Rapid Terra Cotta Project* — For using Gangetic clay in a rapid-modelling process, in order to create computer-controlled 3-D structures for patterns and tools.
- *Khasra-Pengachu Project* — For developing a low-cost computer (on *Pengachu* platform), dedicated to have secure and incorruptible land-records, with sound and picture interfaces.
- *Swara-Gandhar Project* — For developing a low-cost music synthesiser, helpful in retaining the rich heritage of classical music, providing training and composing raga-based music.

Some recent announcements were about the Challan Identification Number (CIN), made mandatory like PAN, — with every payment uniquely identified and resulting in correct credit for payment by every taxpayer. In the outer space, the European Union, 'Galileo' satellite programme — with 30 satellites encircling at medium-level orbits at altitudes around 24,000 km covering the entire earth surface — has been generating for India benefits in sectors like transport, telecommunications, agriculture and fisheries. Sky is literally the limit for IT!

Happy reading of the book ! UTPAL K. BANERJEE

Acknowledgements

Over a long span of nearly four decades, it is difficult to recall every "Good Samaritan" in my life whom I must thank whole-heartedly for their very kind helping hands, but here is the best of a list that I can muster to think:

- Prof. Ken Lomax of UMIST, UK, for steering me through the ordeals of a Ph.D.
- Prof. Ronnie Shephard of Royal Military College of Science, UK, for guiding me into Military or and War Games.
- Richard Mole, dear colleague in Manchester, for taking me through labyrinthine FORTRAN programs.
- Major General A. Balasubramaniam of DoE, for inducing me to join CSI on return from the UK.
- Brig V.M. Sundaram, ex-President, CSI, for being ever helpful.
- Prof HN Mahabala of IIT Kanpur and Chennai, for urging me to write books on IT.
- K. Janardan of Tata Steel, as colleague, for helping me with Programmes Chair at CSI-76, Kolkata.
- Sam Pitroda, the redoubtable technocrat, for always remaining a mentor.
- R.N. Basu, Kishore Budhiraju and A. Suresh, for forming a great team at ASCI.
- Prof. S. Sampath, the Computer Titan, for using my services in UPSC, IIT Kanpur, Defence R&D Organisation and CSI.
- Dr. K.K. Bhutani of J.K. Applied Physics Institute, Allahabad, forever being a help.

- Rohit Chand, for always standing me in good stead.
- Dr. Erling Dessau, Reg. Rep. UNESCO, for letting me consult in regional countries.
- S.L. Rao and P.V.R.N. Iyer, Presidents of AIMA, for being so helpful to me.
- Dr. Kapila Vatsyayan, for being a mentor at IGNCA and always afterwards.
- Col. B.K. Rai, ex-M.D., UPTRON, for being ever so helpful.
- Saurabh Srivastava, ex-XANSA India, for always being helpful.
- Subas Pani, ex-Chief Secretary, Odisha, for using me as advisor to OCAC, Odisha.
- Mohan Tambe, ex-C-DAC and DoE, for being ever endearingly helpful.
- Prof. R.K. Arora of IIT, Delhi, for being ever so helpful.
- Tarun Paul, for being a great colleague at ET&T and Rollatainers.
- Col. Ravi Sharma, for helping in CSI's International Workshop on Rural Development.
- Col. Vinay Khanna, for creating Forum for Information Technology (FIT) with me.
- Kamalini Dutt, ex-Director, DD Archives, for being a great colleague for the official "Leaders of India" project on A-V holdings for India's iconic leaders.
- Pratapanand Jha, Director of CIL, IGNCA, for being a great colleague at IGNCA.
- Dr. N. Ramani, ex-Director, NITIE, for being ever so helpful;
- Dr. Sneh Mohan, Director, CDT, for always being the greatest of help.
- Sonali Choudhry for being a great help in sponsorship and collection of photographs.
- Professors, scholars and academicians of China's premiere universities in Beijing, Nanjing, Shanghai, Dalian and Kunming, who made possible and pleasurable my visits and teaching interactive Post-Graduate courses, with examinations, in China.

Contents

List of Photographs

Introduction

This book is a "first-person, singular-number" account of Indian Information Technology (IT) scene—studded with personal presence of Indira Gandhi, the Dalai Lama, Rajiv Gandhi, the iconic leader Sam Pitroda of India and the father of automation, John Diebold of the USA. Interspersed by many facts and occasional analyses, the colourful scenario began—for me—from management and went to Operations Research (OR) and then reached computers.

It remains primarily a User Viewpoint that observed hardware (HW), software (SW) and computer applications emerge into the Indian arena and bring forth cataclysmic changes in the total scenario, belying all the dire predictions of loss of employment and ultimate doom, and eventually ushering in utility and felicity at an unimaginable level that exceeded even the rosiest of all expectations. It has been, in a nutshell, transition from the "worst of times" to the "best of times", in a true Dickensian sense !

In this transition, mine has been a ring-side view occupied since the mid-sixties. I could see—through "the looking glass"—the earliest genesis of IT and stirrings of its first growth, when it conveyed little sense to managers, executives and administrators—until the time when the cream of decision-makers woke up to the immense potential of the nascent Revolution and its relevance to the decision-making process. By a quirk of circumstances, I could often see, first-hand, some pioneering moments of IT, in a comprehensive sense, such as :

- Proposing a systematic framework for the country's defence management in terms of OR and computers, with several tested and validated, data-based models.

- The setting up of the country's largest computer network, National Informatics Centre (NIC), through the toughest of negotiations with the donor, UNDP.
- Chairing, under the behest of Central Statistical Organisation (CSO), a large inter-ministerial committee to evolve the national commodity classification.
- Participation in the "Futures Study" movement propelled by some Nobel Laureates abroad.
- Earliest contributions in popular writing on computer and management, thanks to the hospitable columns of the *Hindu*.
- Playing a dutiful role, with Computer Society of India (CSI), to usher in fresh thinking in "computer applications for techno-economic development" and "computer applications for rural development".
- Handling of, often single-handedly, the 8-lecture computer module for the senior IAS officers in their 1-week and 4-week "refresher courses", where I had the immense satisfaction of associating myself with one IAS officer out of every three in the country, for induction into the IT revolution.
- Bringing in the first ever Indo-USA video-teleconference on management through dedicated WORLDNET Satellite.
- Nomination as National Project Director by the UNDP for the Indira Gandhi National Centre for the Arts (IGNCA) in setting up their Cultural Informatics Laboratory (CIL).
- Technical evaluation of India SW packages and products, on behalf of ET&T, to enhance their value-added service.
- Working as "Chief Coordinator" for the prestigious, Government of India's "Leaders of India" project for an interactive Website to digitise A-V holdings on Mahatma Gandhi, Jawaharlal Nehru, Indira Gandhi and Rajiv Gandhi.
- Now selected, under the prestigious "Tagore National Fellow" scheme, as "Tagore Research Scholar" for A-V cultural archives of the IGNCA for 2012-14.

While abroad, I was lucky to be :

1. Chairman, for International Federation of Information Processing (IFIP) in Dublin (Ireland) for the industrial

deliberations, alongside the redoubtable Prof. R. Narasimhan on the education side.
2. National Adviser on India for the Asian Productivity Organisation (APO) in Tokyo, Japan.
3. Consultant of United Nations Education, Cultural and Scientific Organisation (UNESCO), to formulate "National Nepal Network" (NNN) in Kathmandu (Nepal).
4. Visiting Professor, three times, to teach full-time Post-Graduate programmes in six top-notch universities in the cities of Beijing, Nanjing, Shanghai, Dalian and Kunming, in China.

Only summaries are cited in the book's narrative. Full details of all involvements, commitments and models of my work would be found in the literature cited in "Bibliography" at the end of the book.

× × ×

My ring-side narrative, I would submit, would make an enticing companion-reading to the excellent monograph, *The Long Revolution: The Birth and Growth of India's IT Industry,* by Dinesh C. Sharma (Harper Collins, ND, 2009). The latter is a nuts-and-bolts history of IT industry in India in a systematic manner, some of whose highlights are cited below :

- Origins of the India IT lay in the vision of a few far-sighted academics and technocrats in the mid-1950s, including Prof. P.C. Mahalanobis at Indian Statistical Institute (ISI), Kolkata, and Dr. Homi Bhabha who set up Tata Institute for Fundamental Research (TIFR) in Mumbai. Prof. Mahalanobis introduced India's first general-purpose computer—the UK-made Hollerith Electronic Computer (HEC) at ISI in 1956, followed by the "Ural" model in 1958 from the Soviet Union. Under Dr. Bhabha, TIFR went for the USA-made IBM 701 system, renamed as TIFR Automatic Calculator (TIFRAC).
- Some indigenous engineers like A.S. Rao of TIFR; V. Rajaraman of IISc, Bangaluru; and Samarendra Mitra of ISI made earlier efforts to build indigenous analog computers.
- Rajaraman, with H.K. Kesavan and H.N. Mahabala, commissioned the first IBM 1620 computer at the newly created IIT, Kanpur in 1964.

- Rajaraman wrote the first textbook, *Principles of Computer Programing* (Prentice-Hall, ND, 1969) at an affordable price of Rs. 15 for students.
- In the early 1960s, the *ad hoc* Electronics Committee under Vikram Sarabhai morphed into Electronics Commission under Prof. M.G.K. Menon in 1971.
- Menon's steering of Electronics Commission was seen by many as a period when roadblocks stalled the growth of IT, with emphasis more on regulation than on development. Delays of 5-7 years were common between applications and their consideration. The government policy—still formulated by political leaders and their bureaucratic advisers—perhaps had a poor understanding of what they were regulating !
- IBM in India in the 1960s and 1970s forced customers—including key public sector bodies like Railways, banks and insurance companies—to install what were essentially second hand systems, rendered obsolete in the West, reconditioned and sold here as new with highly inflated price tags: camouflaged by bundling them into service and maintenance contracts. In one instance in 1975, IBM charged Indian customers $20,000 as the annual rental for a system like IBM 1401, when a similar computer could be internationally bought for $ 1,200 !
- In 1977, IBM was forced to leave India, with the unspoken stance of "after me, the deluge" (a la de Gaul !), underestimating the Indian resolve to ensure that its 100,000 systems would continue to do "business as usual".
- In a rare public-private partnership (PPP), the task of keeping the IBM systems up and running was shared by Computer Maintenance Corporation (CMC), a government entity and International Data Management (IDM), a private group of ex-IBM employees. [Fifteen years had to pass before IBM returned to India in 1999 with a fully-owned Indian entity, sending out a strong signal that India was now a technology power-house, and not geography to dump outdated computers !]
- Rajiv Gandhi had always assumed an unofficial role as a computer-friendly facilitator for events like the 1982 Asian Games in India and smoothed the passage for the major liberalisation that finally came to IT industry in August 1983.

- Soon after Rajiv became Prime Minister in 1984, he announced a new computer policy which, *inter alia*, created Centre for Development of Telematics (C-DOT) in Delhi under Sam Pitroda and Centre for Development of Advanced Computing (C-DAC) in Pune under Vijay Bhatkar. C-DOT transformed, indigenised and upgraded India's archaic telecom system, while C-DAC made India a supercomputing power.
- Post-Rajiv Gandhi in power, there seemed some backlash from the IAS lobby to counter the IT wave since 1989. But N. Vittal, an IAS officer as the new Secretary of DoE, appointed in 1990, reached out for the industry associations, such as, NASSCOM and Manufacturers' Association for Information Technology (MAIT); apprised himself of their "wish list" and set in motion a new wave of liberalisation, including the set-up of state-owned Software Technology Parks (STPs).
- International IT giants like Texas Instruments, Motorola, BOSCH and IBM were allowed to harness satellite technology and set up their development centres in Bangaluru. Videsh Sanchar Nigam Limited (VSNL) was created to provide international data umbilical.
- The IIT model—as epicentre of technology excellence for creating Ph.Ds—did not always reach industry. National Centre for Software technology (NCST) in Mumbai under Dr. S. Ramani repudiated the IIT model and helped to create a generation of earthy engineers.
- Educational area grew when entrepreneurs like R.S. Pawar, Vijay Thadani and P. Rajendran amicably left HCL, the nation's "numero uno" private IT player, HCL, and set up NIIT, in 1981, to impart non-formal computer training for the masses. NIIT was to become one of the world's biggest IT trainers.
- Their parent company, HCL, was born in 1975 when Shiv Nadar and some others left DCM Data Systems, India's first computer-maker, to start their own outfit. For some years, these two companies—joined by ORG and PSI—continued to innovate and provide Indian corporate and lay customers the computer-muscle that complex import regulations still denied.

- In the early 1980s, the HCL Workhorse, as a personal computer, pre-dated the PCs that IBM hardware (HW) and Microsoft software (SW) were to launch jointly almost four years later. The Workhorse used a green-display monitor and five-inch floppy drives to load free SW. HCL had developed clone of WordStar, and their versions of contemporary Database and Spreadsheet SW.
- Sadly, skewed policies made it unviable to manufacture PCs or printers in India. The lack of a strong indigenous HW base continues to hamper the Indian IT industry. SW was another story.
- F.C. Kohli, ex-Tata Electric, helped to build up computer services as independent Tata Consultancy Services (TCS). Azim Premji steered his family vegetable oil business, Western India Products Ltd. (WIPRO) into computers in 1980. Vinay Deshpande gave up a career in Stanford University to start PSI Data Systems in Bangaluru. Deshpande's home in Pune was the office for N.R. Narayana Murthy and five others at Patni Computers, which they left to start, in 1981, their own Infosys Consultants. Today, TCS, Infosys and Wipro straddle the Indian IT scene as "three musketeers" of the outsourced services. [Deshpande, having sold off PSI to a French company, Bull, heads an innovative outfit, Encore, which has a fair share of interesting products.]
- The birth of offshore customer service business was pioneered in 1933 by British Airways, Swissair, Amex and GE, who recognised quite early India's potential for cost-effective technology services. Today, HCL, Wipro and TCS run "call centres" as far apart as Chile and the Philippines.

Sharma's treatise underlines one singular fact: committed people, as much as timely policy, helped turn Indian IT into a respected global brand. Though state's control on the electronics sector is criticised for its dampening effect on the growth of the computer industry, it did help create a huge infrastructure in electronics manufacture in the public sector. The setting up of the DoE, STPs, Centre of Electronics Design and Technology (CEDT) and Technology Missions contributed immensely to the growth of IT, while addressing India's social-sector needs through projects like the

Railways passenger reservation system and the computerisation of the banking sector.

× × ×

Speaking in a lighter vein, Sharma's objective chronicle of doughty generals contributing their mite to Indian IT industry is to be viewed alongside this book's subjective "ballad of a soldier" who was present at the right time at the right place, hopefully for the right purpose! Whether this plucky soldier's contributions could be considered "pioneering", It is left for the readers' piety and judgement.

UTPAL K. BANERJEE

1
Rumblings of IT (1968-72)

A recent blurb in the print media announced rather pithily, "Tomorrow thinks borders are so yesterday". If borders have become so passé for today's giant flying engines manoeuvred by humans—the intended context in the media—deriving their inspiration, then for such a great idea like Information Technology (IT), with its tight bundling of computer hardware (HW) and software (SW), the national and geographical boundaries are becoming even more irrelevant in current times. For, as Victor Hugo had said once, it was precisely "an idea for which time has come": in the middle of the twentieth century, to be precise.

Yet the parameters were nowhere as clear as they now seem in hindsight. My attachment, as a civil-service executive, to Ordnance factory, Khamaria—together with frequent visits to Gun Carriage Factory, Jabalpur and Ordnance Depot, Ranjhi—provided an early insight into the working of the country's powerful defence production and procurement apparatus. Although located in the remotest hinterlands of Madhya Pradesh [Nestling in the pristine wilderness of Kanha National Park and Kisli games sanctuary for wildlife, and with hyenas emitting blood-curdling laughters in the small hours of the night!], the exposure was invaluable, coming as it did as early as 1960-61. Afterwards, when associated with Royal Small Arms Factory, Enfield and Royal Ordnance factories, Blackburn and Chorley, a full decade later in 1969-71, it was apparent how the West was stealing a march in quantitative studies over us in Indian defence, through their Director of Value Engineering, Woolwich, in the UK.

In fact, it was the gamut of analytical studies—the staple as well as the essential prerequisite of all application SW of the latter day computers—that we found lacking among the earlier ground realities. Looking desperately for knowledge in the mid-1960s, we found that we had to turn to the West for the only unambiguous programme of graduate studies in management, run by the British Institute of Management (BIM) from London, with its examination centres at the British Councils in all the Commonwealth countries, with prescribed text and reference books and recommended library work, but no teaching or coaching centres. Interestingly, there was no comparable institutional arrangement for studies in India at that point of time for the middle level executives, let alone any sign of the now familiar plethora of MBA schools or mid-career executive development programmes. A 'Grad-BIM' in 1966 was the earliest coveted graduate degree in management studies that one could acquire by appearing and passing in the overseas examinations in a minimum of 16 papers, in order to qualify for Post-Graduate programmes in the UK. But, only to be fair, while there were academic papers on principles and practice of general management (two of them), personnel management, production management, inventory management, business finance, economics, statistics, psychology, organisation and methods, and several advanced papers,—there was no paper on systems analysis and indeed, operations research was the nearest to what could later qualify for edging near a computer !

In fact, after selection by the Ministry of Education, Government of India, as soon as I landed in the UK for a spell of three years' Ph.D. programme as a 'Commonwealth Scholar'—under the aegis of the Association of Commonwealth Universities (ACU)—in September 1968, University of Manchester Institute of Science and Technology (UMIST) threw open its portals in the Department of Management Sciences to me. At that moment, I was a rank outsider: armed merely with a 'Grad-BIM' degree and civil-service experience of three years (1964-67) as Under Secretary and one year (1967-68) as Deputy Secretary—in Ministry of Defence associated with the General Staff (GS) Branch. This was strengthened by the earlier manufacturing insight in the defence ordnance factories (including 1962-63 at Rifle Factory, Cossipore, and Gun & Shell Factory, Ichhapore, both in West Bengal) and glimpses into the operational aspects of the Indian Army. As luck would have it, Prof. Kenneth Lomax, the well-known statistician heading the department where

I was placed, favoured 'analytical applications of operations research (OR) kind in Indian defence management' as my doctoral dissertation area. Although a closely guarded area, the choice—confined to the academic level assessment and analysis—was providentially suited to my background.

I am mentioning these details to say that defence OR (then better known as Military OR) was, as I gradually discovered, already a highly cultivated domain in the West which was inching towards what would eventually become an accepted part and parcel of IT in course of time,—having a pioneering spirit about itself. But in the beginning, it was easier said than done. There was an enormous leeway to be made up,—in systems analysis, statistics (both parametric and non-parametric), esoteric techniques of OR and even econometrics. The courses were to be sought out and attended, but ample amends were made by such outstanding faculty as Prof. John Johnston (1923-2003) with the aura around him of his classic text-book on *Econometric Methods* and Prof. Brian Moore teaching OR with his over-abundant energy that he liberally shared with one and all.

But the most important feature of learning was interaction with the Regional Computer Centre in Manchester—with its already justifiable fame of developing nascent application SW. Most important of all, there were three computers available: ICL ATLAS, 1905F and 1906A, all of third-generation vintage, with very large scale integration (VLSI) chips just about making their first confident appearance in the computer arena. There was no upper limit on time which we, doctoral students, could go for, and this was a huge boon. FORTRAN-IV, as a programming language (COBOL joined the ranks a little later), had to be learnt by literally racing against time, since computer time was going a-begging meanwhile ! One still remembers the approbation received by writing a successful "calendar" program to predict correctly the week-day for any date-month-year combination: for any time of the distant past and, equally accurately, for any time from the remote future !

But one had also to remain a beast of burden! The data-entry terminals were nowhere in the horizon and one had to carry an awfully large stack of punch-cards to and fro: for handing it over to the console-operator at the centre and again for bringing back the stack to one's work place for detecting—and rectifying—the smallest of glitches that would bedevil one's submission ! The computer hardware was the size of gadgetry filling up large halls, and kept out of bounds from the student community.

× × ×

Soon I realised that Military OR could not be studied in the university alone, but needed exposure to establishments where actual work was being done: mostly with the help of computers. Fortunately, UMIST and ACU concurred with this view and I was allowed attachments and visits for study purposes, and consultations at an academic level, by many institutions and organisations connected with defence management. The following paragraphs will give some idea in a nutshell of my attachments for Military OR in particular and defence management in general.

In the UK (visited in separate spells over 1969-71), Defence Operational Analysis Organisation (DOAO), set up in 1965, directed the OR cells within each service department; the operational analysis (OA) groups with the Fleet Scientific advisers and with Strike, Support, Maintenance and Coastal Commands of RAF; OA groups in Germany and the Far East working directly with Command Headquarters in those areas; and the main OR centre: Defence Operation Analysis Establishment (DOAE), West Byfleet, which allocated 10 per cent of its efforts to studies on each of the three services and 70 per cent to joint-service studies. DOAE concentrated upon the study of complex defence problems, requiring high-level decisions, in the fields of general policy, tactics and strategy, weapon systems, logistic systems, and communications and control. Some interesting features were strategic mobility of the British forces in a European operational theatre by sea and air before and after 1975; war gaming in weapon assessment and resource allocation; and an interesting series of OR studies in finding roots of conflict and crisis management. Other attachments included Road research Laboratory, Crowthorne; Staff College, Camberley; and Controller of Royal Ordnance factories, London and Mottingham.

In the USA (visited in August-September, 1969), an acceptance was found of wide responsibilities and commitments in the international strategic situation and carrying them out with the USA's own resources, with the scale of OR applied to defence as very large indeed. Under the Defense Secretary, Robert McNamara in 1968, the role of some Federal Contract Research Centres (FCRCs) was to conduct "studies and analyses" on behalf the US Defense Department (DOD) and financed by the latter. FCRCs included some small university groups; Mitre and Aerospace Corporations, providing AF with systems engineering capability; MIT, Lincoln Laboratory working for AF and Johns Hopkins Applied Physics Laboratory working for Navy; and OR and SA organisations, namely, Institute for Defense Analyses (IDA), RAND Corporation, Research Analysis Corporation (RAC), Center for Naval Analyses (CNA), and Analytical Services, Inc. (ANSER).

Among the above, I had attachments with US Army Strategic and Tactical Analysis Group (STAG), Bethesda; Case Western Reserve University, Department of OR, Cleveland; RAND Corporation, Santa Monica; IDA, Arlington; and CNA, Arlington,—with the last three operating as not for profit organisations. There were also some profit making OR organisations who were working with the US Defense department, out of whom I liaised with Arthur D'Little, Inc., and the Abt Associates, both in Cambridge, Massachusetts. Most OR work for defence management was hedged with security problems. STAG conducted manual, computer-assisted and computerised war-games lasting from 5 days to 14 months at various command and control levels, to assist in evaluating operational plans and in analysing strategic, tactical and organisational concepts. These included LEGION (a very large battle model); ORION (a logistic network and interdiction system, simulated in SIMSCRIPT); CASCADE (a computerised air-strike and counter air-defence evaluation model); and KATALOG (a computerised information storage and retrieval system).

In Canada (visited in August 1969), I was attached to Defence Analysis Establishment (DRAE), Ottawa, which carried out the main OR functions under the Canadian Department of National Defence (DND). Divided into General Analysis and OR Divisions, they covered strategic OR, mathematics and statistics; logistics analysis, marine OR; land OR; and air OR.

In Federal Republic of Germany (visited in September-October, 1969), the Federal Ministry of Defence (BMVtdg, Bonn) had their OR studies conducted through Industrie-Analagen-betriebe-gesellschaft (IABG, Ottobrunn), a state-subsidised OR enterprise with computers and simulators. IABG ran two groups: Operations research Gruppen (ORG, Ottobrunn) for weapon system analysis and system engineering for the three services; and Zentrate Operations Research

Stelle (ZOR, Trier) for system evaluation for overall defence, and technical and strategic decision-making for the entire ministry. Dynamic Combat Analysis (DYAG) was a comprehensively developed war-game. Study-subjects in OR included scenario studies; weapon systems; support systems; command, communication and information systems; force-structure and allocation problems; central organisation and management; manpower planning; resource analysis, and special application of OR methodology.

In France (visited in September 1969), I was attached to Direction des Recherches et Moyens d'Essais, Paris; Centre Interarmees de Recherche Operationelle, Paris; SROT, Paris; SROM, Paris; and GROAA, Paris. OR studies in French defence management included: operational tactics and strategy, reliability and maintenance, production and inventory, computer for management, concept and management of defence programmes—all under CIRO; weapon system: definition and usage, management of material, personnel and environment—all under SROAT; weapon evaluation, tactics evaluation, statistical evaluation, information and communication problems, material management—all under SROM; operational problems, intelligence problems, logistics problems, personnel problems, administrative problems—all under GROAA.

Apart from the above major countries,, liaisons were made in February 1972 with: Institute of Peace and Conflict Research, Groningen, in Netherlands; Forsvarets Forsknings Institutt, Kjeller, in Norway; Research Institute of Swedish National Defence, Stockholm, in Sweden; and Systems Analysis Committee, University of Helsinki, in Finland.

× × ×

February 1972 also marked the end of the research programme as 'Commonwealth Scholar' for Ph.D., where I made special efforts to include as many as eight case studies: with analytical and computer aided models for Indian defence management. These models—the first of their kinds, validated with real life or simulated data —are conceptually summarised below :

- *India's Defence Expenditure Planning for the Decade 1962 to 1971*: This was analysed obtaining data for India and Pakistan from the *Military Balances* from 1962-63 through to 1971-

72. Inflationary effects were removed at a base-price and "Richardson Process" was applied to detect any "arms race" before major conflict. This was manually done, while a small program in ATLAS AUTOCODE was used for extensive tests on correlation of the various figures, using ICL ATLAS computer.

- *Mobilisation of Manpower Resources in a Variable Situation to Defend Vital Targets*: Briefly, likely operational policies, during transition to tension and combat under various base-situations were considered. Since relevant data would be classified information in any country, realistic data for validating the model was generated from a team of British Army officers—with operational and logistic experience—who were attached for studies to the UMIST in 1970-71. Decision on optimal operational policies, separately for each base, could be tested, which could be quite significant in the context of such mobilisation schemes.
- *Cost Effectiveness Analysis on Air Transportation for Indian Troops and Supplies on UN Peace Missions*: It was necessary to have a set of optimal routes for each available transport aircraft, subject to alternate bases available; wind changing the flight time, "bulking out" (trade-off between volume and weight); base restrictions, ground time to refuel, etc. To compare costs of alternative aircraft systems, the 5-year system-cost technique developed by RAND Corporation was adopted.
- *A Network Analysis for Road Construction in a variable Situation at High Altitudes*: Such constructions were subject to availability of heavy machinery; availability of trained workers; problems of machine performance; problems of climate, geological problems of terrain, and so on. Construction data of east-west Highway in Nepal by Road Research Laboratory, UK, proved to be of help. Out of the heuristic program-packages, RAMPS package developed by CEIR(UK) Ltd; PERT package developed by ICL with a CPM component; and the project cost package by the Department of Civil Engineering, UMIST, were considered, and the third one used after suitable upgradation. The simulated road-construction project network—coupled with the resource allocation scheduling heuristic—helped significantly to gain

insights into the planning, scheduling and control of the project.

- *A Programming Approach to Logistic Build-up in a Variable Situation at High Altitudes*: In such a build-up, the constraints were: time-limits for the tension and combat situations; total weight and bulk of supplies; weight of perishable supplies (by weight and bulk); availability of aircraft crew; and availability of vehicle drivers. The data were processed by a linear programming package, using simplex iterative method, developed with Department of Economic Statistics, University of Manchester, in ATLAS AUTOCODE language and run on ICL ATLAS computer. A very large number of iterations were done to change values of the parameters and to perform sensitivity analysis.
- *A Computerised Simulation for Induction of Troops in a Variable Situation into High Altitudes*: The phenomenon selected for study was the troop induction to four independent (and not inter-connected) high altitude destinations where the formations were located. The questions examined were: what were the overall lift and waiting pattern of the troops so that terminal facilities for reception and quartering could be planned; what were the overall convoy-mobility (and idleness) for POL, maintenance and repairs to be planned; how did each formation expect to fare for arrival, waiting and lift of its troops; and how did the expected usage of vehicles compare among the four routes. General simulation languages like SIMSCRIPT, DYNAMO and GPSS were not easily accessible to the University and, therefore, a generalised simulation code was developed using FORTRAN language. Student's t-distribution tests were performed for sensitivity.
- *A Quantitative Approach to the Generating Variables of Insurgency*: In the first study (April-May, 1970), Delphi Technique was used with participants from the course on "Military Organisation and Modern Warfare" conducted by the Department of Military Studies, University of Manchester. The second study (October, 1970-May, 1971) was conducted incorporating some of the changes suggested in the first one, with participants from the similar course conducted in 1970-71. The technique used a carefully-designed program of sequential individual interrogations, interspersed with

information and opinion feed-back. Study-areas were: Arabia (1916-18); Ireland (1916-21); Cuba (1958-59); China (1939-49); Indo-China (1945-54); and Algeria (1954-62), with participants taken through an information-round on the six areas. The statistical device of principal component analysis was applied to break down the correlation matrix into a set of orthogonal components equal to the number of generating variables concerned. A program was written in FORTRAN language and run with the data on ICL 1905F computer.

- *A Programming Approach to the Regional Planning Framework for Development and Stability in Nagaland*: While the relative lack of economic progress in the State of Nagaland required special efforts to achieve a rapid growth rate, the prevailing political situation demanded special safeguards in priority sectors like communications. A standard program-package for solution of linear programming problems using simplex iterative method, which was developed by the Department of Economic Statistics, University of Manchester, was used, with ATLAS AUTOCODE language and was run several times on a ICL ATLAS computer. With each optimal solution, complete duality and post-optimality analyses were carried out.

On the whole, all the eight case-studies aimed at cardinal measurement of relevant parameters, except for the one for generating variables of insurgency which was primarily concerned with ordinal rank-ordering. The following categories of computer-aided (or completely computerised) techniques were used :

1. *Mathematical Programming*—Regional planning in Nagaland; mobilisation of manpower resources; high-altitude logistic build-up.
2. *Statistical Analysis*—Defence expenditure planning, 1962-72; measurement of generating variables of successful insurgency;
3. *Problem-Solving Heuristics*—High altitude road-building; air transportation to UN Peace Missions.
4. *Monte Carlo Simulation*—High altitude troop induction.

× × ×

While in the UK, I had an opportunity to try out my new knowledge of quantitative management—with or without computer usage—which then was gaining a strong ground all around. In the University of Manchester's neighbourhood (at Sackville Street) was located the Manchester Metropolitan University (till then known as Manchester Polytechnic), where the nascent OR Department had lost its Senior Lecturer Mr. Robson who had suddenly migrated to South Africa ! This happened in the middle of the 1970-71 academic session that was badly affected and the Metropolitan authorities turned to University of Manchester for replacement support. Prof. Lomax suggested that I could take over the assignment. It was an adventurous offer and—out of the dual choice of doing individual OR modules in depth, or, taking up teaching of the whole course—I ventured for the latter. Plunging for the whole gamut was a daunting yet exhilarating task and the process of working out linear programming heuristics and other OR algorithms in the open (and frankly critical) graduate class was not just teaching, but also a learning experience. Even the racial complexion—overwhelmingly white!—was a critical factor and, apart from knowledge of the subject matter, one desperately needed a lot of ready wit and definitely a good sense of humour, to fall back upon. I was very pleased to have possibly passed their litmus test when I found that I was requested to carry on, in the 1971-72 academic session: at both senior lecturer's and examiner's level. It was only with a tinge of regret that I could not continue for long, due to the compulsion to return to my country. But the Metropolitan experience was positively a bonus !

Another bonus was the companionship of some sterling teachers. Prof. Ronald Shepherd of Royal Military College of Science, Shrivenham, Wiltshire, was illuminating in throwing open many mystiques of the defence OR and genially chaperoning me through the mind-boggling Stone Henge at the Wiltshire-Surrey border. Prof' Stafford Beer (1926-2002), consulting in Manchester Business School, and quite a few other academic institutions, already had a formidable international reputation: having formulated principles of cybernetics for management. His cascade of books—mostly from the stables of John Wiley—namely, *Decision and Control* (1966), *Brain of the Firm* (1972), *Designing Freedom* (1974), *Platform for Change* (1975), *the Heart of Enterprise* (1979), *Beyond Dispute* (1994), *et al.*, were tumbling down for the awed readers, one after the other, at that point of time. He accepted me as a deeply personal friend, escorted me to his magical mansion at West Byfleet, full of weird gadgetry and took me up many garden-paths not traversed so far. Most of all, he guided me through the new discipline of cybernetics, inculcating in me a life-long love for the organic (and inorganic) science of negative feed-back of information for gaining the steering control in systems domain.

My last whistle-stop on way back in February 1972 was in St. Petersburg (then Leningrad) where I wanted to look up a professor of the new science of cybernetics in the city's premier university. I sought his telephone number, but discovered to my chagrin that the then Soviet Union did not allow telephone directories to be maintained. The idea, I was told, was that if one knew the person, one would have his number; but if one did not know him, there would be no need of the number anyway ! But the ostensible reason was, I was given to believe, that without a collective directory, there would be no way that people could find out about each other and presumably gang up against the state, or whatever! What a way of maintaining control: cybernetic or otherwise!

I was still buoyed up with enough optimism while returning home, cherishing the idea that the government in general and my civil service authorities in particular would make suitable use of me in applying OR in computer-based studies. Little did I have the inkling of desolation and despair I would be in for, once I was back !

2

Desolation and Despair (1972-73)

Before I embarked on my journey home in February 1972—*via* an exciting land-route across the continental Europe—I was called to Prof. Lomax's office. The venerable professor (he was already known to be suffering from Cancer and unfortunately did not live long thereafter) informed me with a pleasant smile that the Association of Commonwealth Universities was writing to the Defence Secretary, Government of India, that a civil servant has done what they thought was commendable work in the field of OR and computers for Indian defence management and the Indian government should favourably consider implementation of the primary research-outcomes from the doctoral study, which they were forwarding herewith.

I was in the seventh heaven of joy. It was not that I was unhappy with my own research work and the survey of the consanguineous work that was being done in the West, but this was quite an unexpected pat on the back !

Enthused by this encouragement, during my travel home in February 1972, I drew a score board of what I would have gained in the UK and what possibly my concrete contribution would be to my country out of my stint as a "Commonwealth Scholar" in 1968-72. Without making any pronouncements on the fields where my research study could claim to have made contributions to new knowledge in analytical and computer based models—of direct relevance to Indian situation—I could make out the following tentative list of areas where the models developed by me could have perhaps advanced the "state-of-the-art" of existing knowledge :

- Perception of strategic climate between India and hostile neighbours.
- Optimal provision of reinforcements to protect vital targets in a variable situation.
- Evaluating criteria for mine-warfare at high altitudes.
- Highly flexible and integrated land and coastal defence.
- Vulnerability index for air defence.
- Priority index for development projects.
- Trade-off criteria between police, militia and the army.
- Gaming simulation of movements of the insurgents and a changing pattern of information variables.

These apart, the similarity found between modern management patterns and insurgency organisations, and the quantitative measurement of successful insurgency could be said to have contributed a little to new knowledge out of my doctoral research on defence management. Finally, there were also the findings from the eight concrete case-studies (summarised towards the end of Chapter 1).

× × ×

I was returning with much hope that the above features would be looked at for favourable consideration by the authorities, in the light of the request made by the Association of Commonwealth Universities. As I saw in the West, OR, simulation and other statistical and heuristic techniques had been growing there alongside the incipient growth of the computers. In India, in contrast, widening of the OR capabilities towards macro-models—leaving out the post-War days' piecemeal OR studies—was felt desirable, though lacking, at this juncture, with little evidence of application of techniques in the actual decision-making process.

There was an Advisory Group under the Scientific Adviser to Ministry of Defence for introduction of electronic data processing systems (EDPS) in the three services "to improve materially the speed and efficiency of management of personnel, logistics and weapon systems", under which EDPS centres were established in the three services, but there was little evidence of macro-models of OR, simulation and other heuristics being aided by the EDPS. The senior OR scientists and analysts in the Defence R&D Organisation were mainly interested in theoretical work and elaborate modelling, but had apparently little faith in validation, with EDPS providing little support. S.S. Srivastava was a veteran authority on OR but no credence on computers. Even the newly-emerging ideas of cybernetics—with occasional visits and signals of encouragement from Stafford Beer to defence experts like Amitava Ghoshal—veered completely towards theory, as seen from the newly-established journal of *Cybernetics*, edited by Ghoshal. Since OR studies in the West always led to analytical SW as a stepping stone to computer and since I had picked up that combined culture, I tried respectfully to mediate with Srivastava and Ghoshal in the matter, but it was of no avail.

Armed with the exhortations of the Association of Commonwealth Universities, I sought appointment with the Defence Secretary, V. Shankar, in early March 1972. He confirmed having got the ACU missive from the UK; received politely my two bound volumes of research; and gave patient listening to my eager discourse on the potential of OR and computers in decision-making in Indian defence management. I was later told that my research-studies were marked to Mr. Bhatnagar, Director (Planning) in the ministry for "further action". As to whether the analytical models and their validation, presented on a platter, were examined any further—let alone considered for implementation fully or partially—I had no idea, since nobody from the ministry ever contacted me afterwards.

Meanwhile, my civil service authorities posted me in Patna to a career-position of Joint Controller of Defence Accounts (JCDA) for Eastern Command of the army,—with two more transfers at identical levels, but with different responsibilities, first in Allahabad as JCDA (Pensions) and then in Kolkata as JCDA (Factories). These postings, related entirely to accounts matters, were all within a swift spell of one year: with no "connect" to defence management or its decision-making, or to analytical modelling and OR, for that matter. I had to make constantly—though piecemeal—efforts to find my own outlets: to keep a tab on my professional pulse.

My first opportunity was when I extensively toured the Andaman and Nicobar Islands in late 1972 and was fortunate to be given the exclusive support of the ship SS *Teresa* for a round-the-islands sea journey. In that picturesque aquatic landmass, Project Yatrik—under the country's Border Roads Development Organisation—was busy building an arterial road in the Great Nicobar Island, upto the strategic tip of the Pygmalion Point: geographically the furthest southern point for our country (a few kilometres further south in latitude, than Kanya Kumari). At that point of time, the Indian mainland was connected only by weekly sea-fairing vessels form Kolkata and Chennai, other than the Kolkata-Port Blair air route by the Indian Airlines. Getting men, raw material and heavy road building equipment across the high seas and their transportation across the multiple islands were decidedly a Herculean task. I put forward to the authorities a project management approach with network analysis for Yatrik's road building project.

Again, massive efforts were already on to enlarge and modernise the quay side area of the Port Blair Wharf where ships were anchored and unloaded. During my stay, I ventured to propose a detailed project networking approach. I also suggested that it was possible to plan decision making for utilisation of berths, minimisation of time and reduction in cost at the following three stages :

1. The ship arrival pattern, dependent on arrival time and availability of docks in order to enter the ports.
2. Loading and unloading pattern, affecting the stay at the port and dependent on the most economic allocation of resources.
3. Departure pattern, involving delay in docks.

All three ideas were worked out on blueprint format in some details, but none of them had any takers. I was hugely disillusioned to find that what appeared to be clear cut analytical choices for problem solving in all three cases was a virtual non-starter under their given circumstances,—due to an obvious lack of familiarity with modern management practices.

It was not that bad on educational front. During my short stint in Kolkata, I was in touch with the Indian Institute of Management, Calcutta (IIMC) in their new campus at Joka, Diamond Harbour Road. IIMC seemed to be an oasis of excellence in the prevailing wilderness: with its brand of dedicated faculty and highly enthusiastic students. Prof. Ramaswamy P. Iyer was the livewire Director who plugged me in to teach a full-semester course on "Decision and Information—an Analytical Approach". Broadly, I covered :

- Non-parametric Statistics in Decision-making.
- Bayesian Methods and a *posteriori* Analysis.

- "Prisoners' Dilemma" In Non-Zero-Sum Games.
- 'Tit-for-tat' and 'Tat-for-Tit' choices in Game Theory.
- Markovian and Non-Markovian Processes.
- Information based Forecasting Techniques.
- Elements of Cybernetics and Feedback Control.

I found students exceptionally receptive. After the examination and evaluation were over, I was inducted again for teaching at the IIMC a second full-semester course, going by the positive response. This was made into a project-based course and drew heavily on my contacts in the Directorate General of Ordnance Factories (DGOF) for organising the following seven collective projects:

- Computer based Production Management, 1 and 2.
- Computer based Materials Management, 1 and 2.
- Computer based Maintenance Management.
- Computer based Personnel Management.
- Computer based Project Management.

While the course used ordnance factories' data-bases, the computer facilities in the IIMC came handy for data processing by the students. We adopted an interview based evaluation this time. These two courses and their evaluation methods are just to illustrate the desired flexibility in the Indian IIM system.

In any case, the two courses were great morale-boosters for me, since I had lost my heart in the civil services ever permitting me to do anything creative and useful in my own country. Since I was keen to dovetail OR and computers, and there seemed to be no opportunity showing up, I was keen on jumping on another stint for such work abroad. Prof. D.J. White, the famous authority on Decision Theory, had then just left Strathclyde University and joined University of Manchester. Promptly came an offer from him suggesting that I joined under him as post-doctoral fellow. In the mean time, luck intervened and I was selected as Adviser (Information System) in the Ministry of Industry, in its technical wing Directorate General of Technical Development (DGTD). Had this intervention not been there, who knows if I had not landed back in the UK, availing of his large endowment and starting a brand new assignment in a new office which, I was told, he had already earmarked for me! This, however, did not happen and I was plonk in Delhi—instead of Manchester—joining DGTD in mid-1973.

× × ×

Much later, the Indian Council for Social Science Research (ICSSR) gave financial support in 1977 to help publishing my research: eventually in 1980 in the book form, *Operational Analysis and Indian Defence.* Prof. Ken Bowen of University of London, UK, wrote in a review in the *EURO Journal* in 1981 to conclude, "It is a *tour-de-force* as the output of one man's enquiry. As far as I know, no comparable book of advice on military operational analysis exists". A similar sentiment was echoed earlier by K.S. Subramanyam, the noted national security analyst, who was the founder-director of the Institute of Defence Studies and Analysis (IDSA), when he was chairing over a public lecture of mine, on *Analytical Approach to Indian Defence,* at the invitation of India International Centre (IIC), Delhi, on 28 August 1980. He commented, "This is the only text book on defence management in the entire Asian continent".

Times of India (ToI) summarised the presentation on the next day, "Dr. Utpal K. Banerjee, a well-known researcher of India's defence problems, today made a strong plea for an analytical approach to the country's defence plan inputs. In his opinion, systems analysts, with the help of computers and statistical models, could help the country get more value for money in terms of enabling the decision-makers to make the right choices and build the desired defence capability".

ToI's fairly astute reportage went on as follows :

- "He said the operational researchers, using the systems analysis techniques, could provide conceptual and analytical premises for a wide variety of management and planning problems in the context of Indian defence."
- "Listing some areas of application of this approach, he said it could be valuable in deciding whether a deep penetration-strike aircraft, like the Jaguar, should be acquired to fulfil the strategic objectives of the country's defence."
- "It could also be applied with benefit to working out the right mixes for internal and external security in areas like Nagaland."

- "He said it could also be used to decide whether the Navy should use aircraft carriers like the Vikrant or depend on an air-arm based on land."
- "In the building of border roads, deciding back-up and deployment patterns for infantry, armour and artillery too, this approach could prove more cost effective, he argued".
- "He cited some case studies to show how this approach could be effective and profitable. It could help build better vulnerability indices for the air force and help create a deterrent mobility in the deployment of military manpower and equipment."
- "He cited a study of the Nagaland Five-Year plan to show how it was hopelessly out of gear. He said the defence security approach should be in-built into such a plan."
- "Dr. Banerjee wanted the highest level decision makers to be more alive to the importance of the analytical approach. It would give greater confidence and teeth to their decisions."
- "K.S. Subramanyam, while underlining the importance of operational research and the analytical approach in tackling the problems of defence management, felt that the final decisions of the strategic aims of a country's defence were political and had to be taken by political leaders."
- "In his opinion, the extension of the analytical approach to problems of defence was linked with the overall political culture of a country and its applications could increase with the degree of sophistication which that culture required."
- "He said while it was important to urge those concerned to adopt the analytical techniques, India had yet a long way to go in these areas of defence management."
- "Air Chief Marshal P.C. Lal (Retd.), making an observation when the discussion was thrown open to the audience, argued that the analytical approach could not be applied to everything in decision-making in defence. He pointed to the American attempt to rescue hostages in Iran and said while the plan had apparently gone through simulation, it seemed the weather was not taken into account; it failed."
- "He said it would have been impossible to rescue the hostages even if the US helicopters had landed in Teheran. The city was so congested that even in normal conditions, it was impossible to pass through its streets."

- "Responding to a question, Dr. Banerjee said while the chief commander had to take a decision on the spot, the analytical approach obviously could make his decisions more effective in areas for forecasting and planning."

× × ×

Emboldened by the reception of my book in the press (see *The Sunday Statesman,* 13 July, 1980; *The Weekly Mail,* 18 July, 1980; *The Sunday Standard,* 10 August, 1980; and others), and encouraged by the response of distinguished audience at the IIC on 28 August, 1980, I wrote on 24 September, 1980 to Ms. Indira Gandhi, the Hon'ble Prime Minister (PM) of India, seeking an appointment with her to present her my book. R.K. Dhawan, Special Assistant to the PM, promptly replied to give an appointment and 8 October, 1980, became for me a red letter day when PM met me at 8.30 a.m.

I, very briefly, gave her the background of my book, explained its enormous potential for the country and offered my humble services to help my land, She gave very patient listening (on every account she was known to be a keen listener) while leafing through my rather voluminous book with rapt attention, promised to "personally look into it later" and asked me to leave it with her "for doing the needful".

Prime Minister of a country is among its busiest people and Indira Gandhi was surely no exception. I often wondered if it was too presumptuous on my part to hope for a favourable outcome, or any outcome, for that matter. In any case, time passed and absolutely nothing happened. Was 8 October, 1980 for me really a red letter day, after everything was said and done ?

3

United Nations as 'Doubting Tom' (1973-75)

In mid-1973, I was deputed to Delhi and placed as Adviser (Information System) with DGTD, in Ministry of Industry. It was a big relief for me to come near SW for government information systems, if not actually analytical techniques of OR kind. There was a government computer centre of the Department of Statistics: with HONEYWELL-400 computer. DGTD processed monthly production data relating to 97 industries covering about 1,400 large-scale industrial companies registered with DGTD on the government computer system. [By 1979, DGTD had increased the monthly production data to cover about 184 industries, thereby processing information relating to approximately 2,900 companies, which would comprise approximately 80 per cent of the large-scale industrial sector of the country. A BURROUGHS-3800 computer system was selected then, to replace the HONEYWELL-400 computer used for the past decade.]

In a classic case of trust misplaced, Brig. (Retd.) B.J. Shahney, the then DGTD, had reposed his faith in the IIMC for creating an information system for his organisation, who, in turn, deputed Prof. P.S. Duggal for the consultancy work with government. The latter was a genuine academic and an efficient COBOL programer but apparently not a systems analyst. In consequence, he went on using COBOL 'print' programs to convert industry production, industrial license, technology and other input data direct into print-outs and decorated some office rooms and corridors into colourful display-kiosks: serving no other purpose like calculating ratios, patterns and ılow-diagrams and deriving any meaningful insight. Meanwhile, he kept himself genuinely busy in Delhi away from Calcutta [so much so that his suffering students at IIMC had given him a new acronym for DGTD—'Duggal Gone To Delhi'!] and his multi-hued print programs served little purpose other than glorified decoration.

Things had to change, the good professor had to leave and the IIMC substituted Prof. Ramaswamy Iyer, the Director and his colleagues, to take personal charge for damage-control. They veered to the other extreme: of using FORTRAN programing language: suitable for using little data for large calculations, instead of COBOL language: appropriate for large data to do little calculations. The earnest professors put in many man-months—rather than mere man-weeks—of painstaking work to deliver finally meaningful results. It was at those stages that I was brought in to do hand-holding with the successive IIMC teams and try to bring matters back to the control gear.

× × ×

Post-Duggal, while the back-breaking 'restoration' work at DGTD was going on in full swing and the time was fast approaching to bid the IIMC a genial good-bye, the idea was brewing in the early-seventies for a national informatics centre (NIC, though the name was coined later on) in the capital—to link up all the ministries and departments of the Government of India in the form of a computer network for eventually creating an information base for the Central Government. This was part of the national objective of setting up regional computer centres in Delhi, Mumbai, Bhubaneshwar, Bangaluru, Kanpur, Chennai, Hyderabad, Pune and elsewhere. Assistance was sought from the United Nations Development Project (UNDP) for the centres in Mumbai (as an adjunct to TIFR as NCSDCT) and as NIC in Delhi directly under the aegis of Department of Electronics (DoE),—to be possibly located at JNU, but later located independently as NIC.

The aim was to have eventually a large, country-wide data-bank at a three-tier concept. At the *third tier,* there would be a centrally operated data bank at the national capital under DoE, who was mooting the idea. This would have decentralised information-bases—developed on newly emerging mini computers—preferably in the State capitals at the *second tier.* Evidently, the *first-tier* information basis would be the localised information centre at the district headquarters all over the country.

This was an ambitious *three-tier* project for which DoE needed massive funding and manpower, for which sources had to be found. When UNDP was approached for a funding around $ 3.5 millions—a colossal amount for those times—"there lay the rub", in the true *Hamletian* sense. UNDP fielded Dr. Erling Dessau (who fell so much in love with India that he was later happy to have another official stint in India as UNDP's Regional Representative), their senior computer-savvy technocrat from Geneva and Prof. McIntosh, a formidable authority on computer HW and SW from Massachusetts Institute of Technology (MIT), USA. Both Prof. McIntosh and Dr. Dessau believed that while the order of magnitude of proposed funding seemed fine, India lacked woefully in its intellectual capital: which could conceive of information systems, the likes of which could fully occupy such large HW systems to justify UNDP investment. Both of them reportedly expressed grave doubts on this score.

Prof. M.G.K. Menon, the erstwhile Director of the Tata Institute for Fundamental Research (TIFR), Mumbai, had then taken up the cudgels of DoE as its Secretary. His brilliant young TIFR associate, qualified in Physics, was Dr. N. Sheshagiri who, too, had come with him to DoE. Then there was the army technocrat, Col. A. Bala Subrahmaniam (later promoted to Brigadier and finally to Major General). *Yet* the gravity of UNDP's reservation was taken to heart by all and a large number of senior, non-DoE professionals were drawn in for putting in teamwork to counter UNDP's objections and suggesting viable information systems in different areas, including the following:

Information Systems for Agriculture—Dr. K.S. Parikh, Project Director, ISI Planning unit, Dr. B.K. Soni, Director, ICAR; Dr. R.P. Sarkar, Director, Met. Office, Agri. Met. Section, Pune; Sri B.D. Sharma, Director (Statistics), CWPC; Dr. Yayathi, ICAR; Dr. N. Vijayaditya, Electronics Commission.

Information Systems for Science and Technology and Social Sciences—Dr. Utpal K. Banerjee, DGTD; Shri P.K. Bhargava, DoE; Dr. Ashok Khosla, DST; Prof. R.C. Nigam, DST; Dr. Ramashray Ray, ICSSR; Shri Baldev Singh, CSIR; Prof. P. Duggal, IIMC (associated upto June 1974).

Information Systems for Industry—Shri D.K. Kundu, CWPC; Dr. R.K. Vepa, DoE; Shri G. Soni, DoE; Dr. P. Chandrasekar, Electronics Commission; Shri P.K. Srivastava, DoE; Shri N.G. Basak, Shri K.N. Ramaswamy, Shri M.S.Grover, Shri Ashwini Kumar,

Shri R.P. Upadhyay and Shri G.G. Jain (All six from DGTD). Information Systems for Technology Development—Shri S. Parthasarathy, INSDOC; Shri S. Mohan, CSIR; Dr H.R. Bhojwani, CSIR.

Information Systems for Social Sciences—Shri S.K. Nizhavan, ICSSR; Shri D.N. Shetha, Centre for Study of Developing Societies; Dr. P. Ramachandran, TISC, Bombay; Prof H.S. Gore, TISC; Prof. V.R. Panchmukhi, Department of Economics, University of Bombay; Dr. D.B. Sardesai, Gokhale Institute of Economics and Politics, Pune.

Manpower Planning—Dr. Nalla Gounden, JNU; Dr Satsangi, IIT Delhi; Dr. Nabaneethan, Institute of Applied Manpower Research; Dr. D. Sankarnarayanan, Addl. Secy., UGC; Shri P.N. Krishnamurthy DoE; R.M. Nair, CSIR.

The major final reports crystallised from the following, among the others :

- Dr. Kirit Parikh, the eminent economist and agro-scientist from Indian Statistical Institute (ISI)—Agricultural Resource Information System.
- Prof. Nabaneethan, from Institute of Applied Manpower Research (IAMR)—Human Resource Information System.
- Dr. Utpal K. Banerjee, Adviser (Information System), DGTD—Information Systems for Industry, for Social Sciences, and for Science & Technology.

× × ×

To illustrate *National Information System for Industry*, in consonance with other management information systems (MIS), it was visualised to comprise: general historical records and communication functions. On one side, raw (or reduced) data and partly processed information could be obtained from various historical records and transmitted to general data bank according to established procedures or on demand. On the other side, output reports—in the form of information analysis—could be formulated by using the reduced data from the general records and transmitted to the individual operational divisions of the industry: as a means to briefing the decision-makers and helping them to coordinate their intelligence and actions.

In other words, general historical records as a repository of formal information could be used by the top management in planning, controlling and coordinating the activities of the industrial organisation,—for instance, the rapid information analysis report in the organisation of the DGTD.

Main features of the decision-flow could be viewed as follows :

- Industries listed and their normal and special features identified.
- Information flow, as within the industry, studied to explain both general historic process and also the communication functions that needed to be created.
- Environments (as functional departments/divisions) selected.
- Objectives for each organised activity in an environment listed.
- Objective-wise *performance indicators* formulated on quantitative basis.
- Objective-wise *standard norms* obtained from past knowledge and experience.
- For each environment, objective-wise formats for output reports prepared, comprising both *performance indicators* and *standard norms*.
- Input data identified at appropriate aggregate levels which would help generate the output reports in the designed proforma.
- Formats prepared for collection and storage of input data.
- Source documents specified from which input data were to be collected.
- Computer-based systems designed and developed, and programs specified.
- Programs coded both for building up and updating the database, and for generating the output information reports.
- At every stage, provision kept for updating of objectives and environments, etc., so that the information system could remain flexible and cope with extraneous changes.

Obviously, a national information system was to be gradually developed for individual industries, In order to show such a potential, we chose the following four industries for developing an integrated information system project for each, covering all aspects: Cement; Electronics; Fertilisers; Power.

For *Cement,* Portland cement manufacturing process (both wet and dry) was chosen in order to give an idea of the industry: from the receipt of raw materials up to packing and loading for distribution. While India did not depend on foreign technology in cement, there was a continuous evolution from the wet to the dry process for increasing the existing productivity. Imports in the case of cement industry were restricted only to cement machinery, and some components and spare parts, while manufacture of cement took place on self-reliant basis. Environments, objectives and indicators for cement industry were drawn out. End-users of the information system were visualised as: the Ministry of Planning, Ministry of Industry, and the concerned administrative ministry.

For *Electronics,* the following main classifications issued by the Electronics Commission were based on an alpha-numeric system :

- Component electronics —
  1. Active components;
  2. Passive components, except electro-mechanical;
  3. Electro-mechanical components; and
  4. Microwave components and HW.
- Mass electronics —
  1. Consumer electronics; and
  2. Mass communications equipment.
- Communications electronics —
  1. Telecommunications equipment; and
  2. Radar and navigational equipment.
- Automation electronics —
  1. Computers and related equipment;
  2. Process control equipment; and
  3. Industrial electronics.
- Instrumentation electronics —
  1. Test and measuring instruments;
  2. Medical electronics equipment; and
  3. Nuclear instruments and equipment.

Environments, objectives and indicators for electronics industry were drawn out. End-users were visualised as: the Ministry of Planning, Ministry of Industry, DoE and partially Railway Board.

For *Fertilisers,* the following types were seen to be used in India:

- *Phosphatic*—Partly indigenously produced. Raw material was both indigenous and imported;
- *Nitrogenous*—Partly indigenously produced. Raw material was both indigenous and imported; and
- *Potash*—Fully imported.

Environments, objectives and indicators for fertiliser industry were drawn following a common pattern. End-users were visualised as the Ministry of Planning, Ministry of Industry, Ministry of Agriculture and the concerned administrative ministry.

For *Power*, the main environments were generation, transmission and distribution. In India, power was produced from coal, oil, gas, natural steam, water and Uranium-235,—comprising thermal, hydroelectric and nuclear. The main goals of power industry were:

- to deliver power at the cheapest rate at given reliability to specified destinations;
- to optimise plant-location; and
- to optimise hydroelectric-thermal-nuclear mix for power.

Environments, objectives and indicators for power industry were drawn, keeping in view generation, transmission and distribution parameters. End-users were visualised as: the Ministry of Planning, Ministry of Industry, Ministry of Steel, Coal and Mines, and Ministry of Energy.

× × ×

To illustrate *National Information System for Social Sciences*, major problems peculiar to Indian situation, as seen by the Indian Council of Social Science Research (ICSSR), were as follows:

- Shortage of trained manpower;
- Limited access to data produced by major data-producing agencies;
- Non-availability of specified data-formats from which data could be easily utilised; and
- Limited access to computing and software facilities for social science data processing.

In keeping with the ICSSR's laid down programme of data archives—to acquire, organise and manage data-sets relating to social science research, and to acquire and develop computer programs to facilitate social science data processing, within the parameters of enhanced training, liaison, consultancy and collaboration—one had to take into account the general historical records as well as the need of communication of relevant results and findings to the decision-makers.

General historical records fell under *primary information* and *secondary information. Primary information* came from directly sponsored and variously funded projects of the ICSSR. *Secondary information*, originally meant for use elsewhere but also valid for social science research, came from :

- *Registrar General of India* (responsible for Census data)—Literacy; religion; sex; migration; occupation structure; etc.
- *National Sample Survey Organisation* (30 rounds of survey till then)—Household composition; consumer expenditure, capital formation, transport facilities; land holdings; etc.
- *Reserve Bank of India*—Rural credit survey; cost-benefit studies; field studies; banking facilities; determination of norms; etc.
- *Commissioner of Scheduled Castes (SC) and Scheduled Tribes (ST)*—Reservation in services; educational development; eradication of untouchability; protective legislation; etc.
- *Directorate of Economics and Statistics, Ministry of Agriculture*—Cultivation costs of principal crops; agro-economic research coordination; crop estimation surveys; *ad hoc* agricultural and livestock census (under FAO); market intelligence assessment; etc.

Communication functions were the quantitative measures for deriving processed information from the raw social research data in as systematic and condensed manner as possible and their distribution to the decision-makers in different central ministries, departments and divisions and various directorates in the Central and State Governments; Planning Commission; and guiding social science researchers.

Illustrative exercises were undertaken for identifying simple *information indicators* and deriving compound *information indicators* from a few social science research projects from the following social science centres,—based on the evaluating criteria of national importance; capability of being pulled together; inter-disciplinary nature; and sufficient urgency.

- *The Centre for Study of Developing Societies, Delhi* —
  1. General Elections in India: 1967; 1989 (mid-term elections); and 1971.
- *The Tata Institute of Social Sciences, Mumbai* —
  1. Sociology of education;
  2. Study of SC and ST students at schools and colleges;
  3. Family composition studies;
  4. Professional social workers in India—employment position; and
  5. Village profile.
- *The University of Bombay, Department of Economics, Mumbai*—
  1. Evaluation of land reforms;
  2. Urban labour market with reference to Mumbai;
  3. Analysis of trade policies in India;
  4. Linkages and industrialisation in the ECAFE countries;
  5. Exports from India under the General Scheme of Preference;
  6. Inter-regional planning model for trade for trade cooperation in ECAFE countries;
  7. 'Economies of scale in the Indian manufacturing industry;
  8. Effects of public expenditure with reference to education and health; and
  9. Evaluation of Indian fiscal system.
- *The Gokhale Institute of Politics and Economics, Pune* —
  1. Construction of an input-output table for India, 1963;
  2. Land resources in relation to population in India;
  3. Compilation of forest resources in a State like Maharashtra;
  4. Income, saving, and investment in a district like Ahmednagar;
  5. Evaluation of Small Farms Development Agencies (SFDA) in a district like Mysore;
  6. Socio-economic studies of SC in a rural area as in Maharashtra;
  7. Crash scheme for rural employment and evaluation of programmes in a district like Satara;

8. Impact of assistance under PL-480 on Indian economy;
9. Youth policy in a State like Maharashtra;
10. Progress of literacy in villages in a State like Maharashtra; and
11. Exploitation of forests through forest labour cooperatives.

Statistical tests on sample size, sample reliability, sample homogeneity and sample environment were recommended by social science research scholars with quantitative background.

× × ×

To illustrate *National Information System for Science and Technology*, the 1973 policy of National Committee on Science and Technology (NCST) had visualised provision of a national information service, with optimum utilisation of existing information services, promotion of cooperation on information exchange and development of facilities enhancing information services. This would be within a framework of national centres (NCs), regional centres (RCs), and branch centres (BCs) of information at hierarchical levels, ending with local information units (LIUs) at the lowest level of individual R&D establishments.

Users in industrial and technological fields needed selected data of practical importance: as digested, for direct assimilation; as analysed in detail, for application to specific problems; and as culled out from source documents for timely use. The data-bank structure was outlined in the following sequence:

- Division of industrial and technological fields into 24 sectors (identified in the Science and Technology Plan), then into areas and finally into specific projects—for product or process development;
- Identification of the needs and priorities in technology development based on India's investment policies (technology needs and priorities);
- Enlisting of technological alternatives for specific projects (technology forecasting);
- Monitoring of foreign technologies appropriate for India (technology monitoring);
- Selection of Indian technologies suitable for nurturing and potential application (technology assessment);

- Identification of technology gaps and agencies, and funding assistance for the development work (technology planning);
- Establishing of mechanism for efficient transfer of know-how (technology transfer); and
- Keeping track of utilisation of know-how in practice (technology utilisation).

Allowing for some overlapping, fairly independent information systems could be structured around sub-data bases as follows:

1. Sub-data base on technology needs and priorities;
2. Sub-data base on technology forecasting and monitoring;
3. Sub-data base on technology assessment and planning; and
4. Sub-data base on technology transfer and utilisation.

Each sub-data base could be on a low-cost mini-computer under the control of the organisation which would be the natural focus for collection, storage and processing of the specified system as follows:

- *Sub-Data Base on Technology Needs and Priorities —*
  For technology demands and enlisting priorities,—linking Customs, Reserve Bank of India; DGTD and SIDO (Small-Scale Industrial Organisation),—with mini-computer possibly located at DGTD or Planning Commission.
- *Sub-Data Base on Technology Forecasting and Monitoring —*
  For technology supply and determining technology alternatives,—linking professional literature and trade journals; expert panels, administrative ministries, Department of Science and Technology (DST); commercial attaches in Indian Embassies/High Commissions; international agencies,—with mini-computer possibly located at DST.
- *Sub-Data Base on Technology Assessment and Planning —*
  For technology gaps and development options,—linking Atomic Energy labs: Space labs; IITs, IISc, private labs; ICAR labs; ICMR labs; CSIR labs; DRDO labs; Irrigation labs; P&T labs; Railways labs; Energy labs, —with mini-computers possibly located at CSIR, ICAR, etc., headquarters, on a mini-computer network.
- *Sub-Data Base on Technology Transfer and Utilisation —*
  For the end-use of technology and transfer of developed

technology to industry,—linking international funding and developing agencies (UNDP, UNIDO, UNCTAD); 'technology transfer centre'; DST; NRDC (National Research Development Corporation); national funding and developing agencies; administrative ministries,—with mini-computer possibly located at NRDC.

The scheme, as outlined, was capable of having the following interfaces in technology data-bank:

- Interface between technology forecast and technology in the "pipeline" (finished and in the laboratories);
- Detailed appraisal on forecast and forthcoming technologies;
- Summarised reports on industry's needs of current and future technologies;
- Interface between technology in the pipeline and technology implemented;
- Interface between technology commercialised and technology in the pipeline;
- Interface between technology forecast and technology commercialised;
- Interface between technology forecast and technology implemented;
- Interface between technology commercialised and technology implemented;
- Detailed appraisal on commercial and productive technologies; and
- Summarised reports on commercial and productive technologies.

× × ×

The above three national information system projects, among all others, evidently satisfied the "doubting Toms" among the UNDP, for the project got approved and the large three-tier computer system came through with flying colours! [The National Informatics Centre (NIC) was christened as such by Erling Dessau of UNDP, who preferred the French name of "Informatics" to the emerging American alternative, "Information Technology", although the latter has proven more robust over the years!]

NIC, once established, was put under the stewardship of Dr. Sheshagiri and met its promise very well, linking up nearly a dozen departments of the Government of India by May 1977. Gradually, NIC connected 50 to 60 mini-computers—one to each department of the Government of India—to its own $3.5 million front-end computer, HP 21 MX, as the host system. With its 40 post-doctoral specialists in electronics and computer science,, and as many M. Techs., it rapidly developed competence for the HW (operation, maintenance and enhancement, when due), SW and inter-connections. NIC established a thorough capability as was evident from their obtaining in 1977 a $1 million software/hardware export contract from the USA.

By May 1979, computing needs of the Central Government ministries and departments were proposed to be met through the large computer system of the NIC; the computer centre under the Department of Statistics; and the computer system at the Planning Commission. The latter installed an Inter-Data 8/32 computer in February 1978. While DGTD was supported by the Burroughs 3,800 computer system at the Department of Statistics, NIC supported the Development Commissioner, Small Scale Industries (DCSSI) in developing information system for small-scale industrial units. As mentioned, mini-computer terminals in various government departments were interlinked to the large NIC system by means of communication links. NIC installed and commissioned in August 1980 a large host computer, CYBER 170/720 system of the Control Data Corporation, USA,—with further assistance from the UNDP. The system consisted of a dual central processing unit, 196 K-word memory (60-bit word), 2.5 billion bytes of disc storage, nine tape drives, two line printers, two card readers, one batch terminal, three network processing units, 30 terminals and one system console. This was the biggest computer system in the country in 1980,—to give an idea of the state-of-the-art at that point of time. Interestingly, the system was already earmarked for further expansion in 1983-84, which also illustrated the rapid evolution of the technology.

By 1979-end, computerisation services were given to 18 departments/organisations of the government. Supplementary regional facilities at a minimal level were established by 1981 at NIC cells in Mumbai, Kolkata and Chennai. Similar regional facilities were established in Chandigarh, Pune and Roorkee afterwards. These projects provided regional availability of computer services to all as well as computer network infrastructure for information-sharing among various departments/organisations, thereby avoiding duplication of efforts.

Up to 1981, minicomputer terminals were fully commissioned at end-user locations, namely, National Council of Educational Research and Training (NCERT); National Institute of Health and Family Welfare (NIHFW); ICSSR, Registrar General (Census) of India; Indian National Scientific Documentation Centre (INSDOC); computers at geographical locations like Shastri Bhavan; Nirman Bhavan, Krishi Bhavan and Sardar Patel Bhavan; and an optical document reading facility at UPSC.

With the responsibility to assist the user departments in the development of computerised information systems, NIC established intra-city computer network in Delhi,—by connecting the mini-computer terminals to the host CYBER computer system being leased telephone lines and radio (VHR) frequencies. With a view to building up an inter-city network, NIC conducted Delhi-Ahmedabad satellite data communication experiment, using APPLE satellite in 1981.To assist departments in analysing performance data for taking policy decisions, NIC developed 50 information systems by 1982.

× × ×

Under Rajiv Gandhi's remarkable initiative (though not in power), the IX Asian Games in 1982 were staged with computerised information systems playing a unique role to cover the following aspects:

- Past Asian, Commonwealth and Olympic results tally;
- Current Asiad results;
- Accreditation and accommodation;
- Village resident status;
- Stadium construction monitoring;
- Personnel selection; and
- Ticket accounts consolidation.

On results of previous games, free-format queries—with answers containing full details of event, game, year, winning country, medal, name and performance details—was another novel feature for the Asiad, as per the following samples:

1. Give details of medals won by India in Men's Hockey in Asian games;
2. Give men's 100 m sprint gold medals in the last three Asiads;
3. Give the performance of India, Pakistan and Korea in Football in the past Asian games;
4. When did Japan win the first Olympic gold?
5. Which India wrestlers won medals in the last two Asian games?

On result information system, free-format queries could be as per following samples:

1. Give results of the heats of men's 2000 m sprint held on a particular date;
2. With whom is India next scheduled to play in Football ?
3. In which stadiums are the Malaysians competing today ?
4. Winners of 100 m Sprints for men?
5. Results of matches played between country 'A' *versus* country 'B' in a given sport/game;
6. Record set in the current Asiad, if any (with information on latest world/Olympic records, etc.); and
7. Medal tally position—country-wise, event-wise, day-wise—as of date.

On accreditation and accommodation details, free format could use any combination of the attributes, such as: name; ID No.; country; sport; event; function; accommodation; back No.; sex; date of birth; date of arrival; and date of departure. Free-format queries could be sampled as follows:

1. How big was the Japanese contingent ?
2. In which Athletic event are the Malaysians taking part ?
3. How many Indonesian competitors were staying in the village today ?
4. What was the weight of the Korean boxer with Back No. 10 ?
5. How many women gymnasts were there with age below 20 years ?

Free-format queries came galore and were the real fun for the spectators, onlookers and game-lovers alike. But only they could test the strength and scope, tenacity and versatility of NIC's computerised games information system: to earn enough applause !

× × ×

As a post-script, one could highlight the felt need and evolution of common commodity classification, long felt not only in India, but also in advanced countries like the USA and the UK. Prof. Wassily Leontief (1901-1999), the Russian input-output economist and Nobel laureate in 1973, voiced the common concern by saying: *The spectacular advances in computer technology increased the economists' potential ability to make effective analytical use of large sets of detailed data. What are, however, urgently needed are the establishment, maintenance and enforcement of coordinated uniform classification system. Incompatible data are useless data...*

The Statistical Commission of the United Nations Economic and Social Council (ECOSOC) prepared, over 1971-74, international classification of goods and services (ICGS) to play a specific role in overcoming difficulties mentioned by Prof. Leontief. In India, ICGS was taken note of by the Central Statistical Organisation (CSO) under Ministry of Planning, in order to evolve a common commodity classification as follows:

- To use the rationale in the ICGS reflecting the latest thinking in industrial classification; and
- To provide a common base to various government agencies for goods and services of industrial origin.

Accordingly, CSO set up in June 1974 a working group under my chairmanship with a view to evolving such a classification, with representatives from CSO, DGTD, DGSD, P&T Department, Department of Company Affairs, DoE, Ministry of Defence, Ministry of Agriculture, Railway Board and other ministries and departments co-opted from time to time. The group was asked, to start with, to adopt the present National Industrial Code (NIC-70) as a base and extend it to six-digit or eight-digit level so as to cover major industrial commodities, looked after by various organisations in the country.

As a first step, we found necessary to consider some changes essential in NIC-70 in order to make it more rational, comprehensive and up-to-date. At the next stage, NIC-70 was extended to cover industrial commodities (products and sub-products) with the following aims:

1. To ensure comprehensiveness of NIC-70 at four-digit level for each industry;
2. To cover individual commodities at the six-digit or eight-digit level as per the principles of ICGS;
3. To ensure that the coverage as above caters for the government needs;
4. To allow ministries and departments to come over to the national commodity classification, as above, on a gradual basis; and
5. To allow other ministries and departments, unable to do so, to build up concordance between own systems and the common classification system.

It was significant that almost all ministries and departments found the above aims acceptable and decided to correlate to it. Two specific points emerged during our work and found generally acceptable to all :

- Along with the commodity classification, there was a need for standardisation in the commodity *nomenclature*, to ensure that the same nomenclature is used by all concerned for a specified commodity; and
- In addition, there was a need for suggesting standard *accounting units*. For instance, the "production capacity" of a crane-producing concern could be either "number of cranes" or "tonnage of cranes" or "monetary cost of producing the cranes". In the absence of standard accounting unit, it would be difficult to follow the progress in "production" of the above concern from year to year !

4

Exploration and Experimentation in IT (1975-78)

In mid-March of 1975, I went to meet the XIV Dalai Lama up in the Himalayas. But thereupon hangs a tale.

Civil Services in general—and my own service in particular—did not look kindly upon the attempt at specialisation, even though it might be very much in the interest of the country. OR and computers were just dawning on the land's horizon, and the early-morning haze of such specialities was seen with profound distrust. [After I had left the shores of my land, I believe my authorities fathomed that the sponsorship for my being "Commonwealth Scholar" was a huge mistake. To start with, they reportedly took my administrative boss to task for having signed the relevant certificate giving me clearance. Then, they proceeded to write to the Association of Commonwealth Universities, UK, that I was not really "sponsored" and could they be so kind as to send be back to India. I understand that a polite reply was sent back to say that my service "sponsorship" made little difference to the UK authorities, that they were reasonably happy with my academic progress, that they would continue to pay me the promised scholarship, and that I would be asked to return to my country only after my mission was accomplished. I, of course, was kept in the dark about these "developments" and was "enlightened" long after my return.]

In March 1975, my three years' "bond"—which was taken from me before I had left country, stipulating that I would continue to serve for a minimum of three years on return or pay back the scholarship-money to the government—was due to expire. Again, I was told that this "bond" was a bit of a charade, because the scholarship money was not paid by our government and, therefore, the latter had no legal hold on it. I was further told of other "Commonwealth Scholars" who had merrily stayed back, or, returned early abroad, and the signed "bonds" could make precious little difference for them, legal or otherwise. Be that as it may, I was in the government for the entire "bond" period, before I had a providentially sent call from the famed Bombay House at the Fort, Mumbai—of the House of the Tatas—querying if I would be interested for a professional position and would wish to join the Tata Steel in Jamshedpur: as their Divisional Head of Manager, Management Services.

It was much more than a mid-career decision. It was a change from the settled and unshakeable comforts of a superior civil service to the uncertain stakes of professional corporate management. It was also a change from the magic and charm of the country's multi-coloured capital to the fabled, but essentially monochrome, steel city, built by Jamshedji Nusserbhanji Tata seven decades ago,—where one had to live and eat, sleep and dream "iron and steel" all the time!

In Delhi's sun-soaked March morning of 1975, I decided—entirely on an impulse—to go to the Himalayas and to seek the Dalai Lama's pious advice on what I should really do. I landed in Dharamshala without an iota of idea if he was present there. Yes, I was lucky he was; but a "holy audience" was not available in another three months. Then suddenly the telephone rang at the Tourist Lodge (where I was staying, literally sulking !) to convey the sudden cancellation of an afternoon appointment and urging if I could climb up to his private abode at Macleodgunj: over a thousand feet high: to see him in about an hour. The impossible was done. When I put forth my dilemma to him and sought his blessing, the Dalai Lama responded—as a truly noble soul—"I will pray for you". I was intensely touched and trusted those prayers would abide by me all the while.

[There was a sequel. I resolved to pay him my intellectual debt of gratitude and consecrate him an appropriate book, if and when I could write one. The opportunity came in 2007-09 when I was awarded a Senior Fellowship by Ministry of Culture, Government of India, and completed my two-volume comprehensive work, *A Journey with the Buddha,* dedicating it to the Dalai Lama and handing him over my first set personally at the International Guest House, University of Delhi, in August 2010. It gave me immense satisfaction that he received my two volumes with the warmest of smiles and earnestly wanted to publicly release my book. This was, however, never to be.]

× × ×

When I landed in Jamshedpur at the end of March, 1975, I was put in divisional charge of Management Services, comprising EDP department with two second-generation IBM 1401 computers, OR department and Statistics department,—equipped with systems analysts, programers, OR analysts, statisticians and support manpower. There was also a constant interaction process with Industrial Engineering (IE) department, and Organisations and Methods (O&M) department.

By then, we had become well aware that the world-view and science of the *Machine Age* was ending and the new world-view was emerging pre-occupied with *Systems*. Let me explain. According to Russell Ackoff (1919-2009)—the celebrated founder of *INTERACT* at Wharton School of Pennsylvania State University—man's attention shifted from death to life and the world in which it took place at the time of Renaissance. Use of *analysis* was the dominant mode of thought which began with the *Machine Age* then. Relationships of cause and effect, yielding a deterministic concept of the universe—helped to organise the world-view and science of the *Machine Age*.

According to Ackoff, World War II had marked the beginning of the end of the *Machine Age*. Formulation of a new world-view was brought about by the pre-occupation with *systems*, their growing complexity, and the increasing difficulty of managing them effectively. The realisation that *systems* were wholes which lost their essential properties when taken apart, led to an understanding in terms of the system's role and function,—which went beyond the analytical knowledge of the system's structure.

The above systems thinking—based on expansionism and non-deterministic causality—had provided the foundation of the *Systems Age*, whose world-view incorporated the Machine Age as a special case. Machines began to be understood as instruments of purposeful systems, but not the purposeful systems conceptualised as machines. Ackoff viewed the post-industrial revolution as a logical consequence of systems thinking, as the industrial revolution was of mechanical thinking. In this second revolution, man sought to develop and use instruments that would do mental work rather than physical work,—

artefacts that would *observe* (generate symbols), *communicate* (transmit symbols) and *think* (process symbols logically). Together, these technologies made possible the mechanisation of *control and automation.*

In a unique way, the Tata Steel in Jamshedpur was way ahead of the Machine Age because of its formulation, from the beginning, as an integrated steel plant, but it fell short of the Systems Age due to its lack of process-control instrumentation—awaiting the arrival of the third and fourth generation micro-processors—that could lead to mechanised control and automation.

The integrated steel plant operated right from the raw materials stage unto the final products stage,—with the production treated as an integrated process where *output* of the previous process was treated as the *input* of the subsequent process.

- The entire process began from the acquisition of coking coal and non-coking coal from the "captive" collieries (under Tata's ownership) and the "non-captive" coal-mines (under the Coal India's ownership) from both of which the coal carrier wagons reached the plant in a "round-robin" fashion, that is, wagons getting unloaded in the plant, released, getting back in the circuit for being loaded at the mines and put back in the transportation network over again. Since the coking and non-coking coal had varying ash-content (with sulphur and phosphorus) and volatility, optimal coal-blending to achieve desired levels of ash as well as volatility was an OR exercise that could be introduced.
- The series of Coke Ovens carried out the "caking" process: for extruding the ash and enhancing the carbon-content for the coal-burning efficiency. This needed a watch on the "coke-rate" which was kept under constant statistical monitoring.
- The five Blast Furnaces contributed to iron-making and formed a crucial component of the throughput that determined the entire quality of the subsequent steel-making: right up to the final product stage. The mechanised pouring from the top of raw iron ore—another blended product after acquisition from different iron mines—and their calibrated burning through gigantic funnels with the blasting of the coke ovens mix of gas and coal was an agonising process where

only sensitive manual skills could operate a semblance of control, in the absence of the later-day process instrumentation. "Iron-to-Steel ratio" was another quantitative parameter kept under constant check.

- Pouring of the "hot metal" (liquid iron) from the bottom of the Blast Furnaces on to the ladles was done every three-to-four hours. [This periodic "tapping", incidentally, made an unforgettable sight from above and especially from the high Dalma Hills at some distance: emblazoning the whole sky, particularly at night, with a deep hue of crimson-red.] Empty ladles were lined up for this purpose and their transportation to the three nearby Steel Melting Shops (SMS) could form a classic "queuing" algorithm: arrival-pattern of ladles; service time (for "tapping") and departure-pattern for the SMSs.
- Three SMSs were earmarked for converting hot metal into finished steel, by pouring some additives. Finished steel was collected in the ingot moulds. SMS laboratories did the quality-classification among the finished steel ingot moulds. There was also "scrap" left of a low residual value: either to be recycled into steel-making or to be disposed of as scrap of negligible value. Optimisation (for minimal quantity) of scrap disposal was an OR exercise, worth several crores of rupees, on a periodic basis.
- Steel ingots branched off from the SMSs into the two Rolling Mills. Rolling Mill I was a Blooming Mill,—leading to blooms being pressed as wheels and axles. Rolling Mill II was a Billet Mill,—leading to billets being cut, tapered and drawn into rails and at times into wire-rods. Automatic billet-cutting according to prior planning—that could be altered at specific time-intervals—was an important variable to be controlled by instrumentation, whose efficacy had to be judged from the minimisation of "rejections", i.e., the billet-ends scrapped. The same considerations applied to blooms, *mutatis mutandis*, for their "rejections".
- From Rolling Mills I and II—responsible for the most important throughputs, namely, blooms and billets—It was a downhill process of crafting end-products through various mills, like Wheel Mill, Axle Mill, Rail Mill, Wire-Rod Mill, and so on. At every finishing mill, the minimisation of

"rejections" was an important consideration affecting vitally the product-profitability.

The above process-flow in the integrated steel plant would give some idea as to how throughput at various flow-points could be analysed to get the company best value for money—using OR and computer capability at our disposal. Three innovative exercises undertaken were :

1. *Billet Profitability*—Since billets were throughputs for a large range of end-products, a profitability analysis was undertaken to determine which categories of billets the Tata Steel should concentrate upon for attaining highest profits, within the upper and lower bounds of market-demand.
2. *Rejection Analysis*—Since there was stage-wise rejection, the end-point rejection was made the starting point and then worked backwards at every stage of the throughput, to determine how total rejection-value could be pegged to the minimum, within a given range of market-demand.
3. *Computerisation of on-going Statistical Reports*—A large variety of statistical reports that were manually produced every month was later generated by computer,—after first creating the permanent statistical data-base and then generating the variations every month, and incorporating reasons therefor, wherever feasible.

× × ×

While it was a pleasure to function as the Divisional Manager of Management Services of the Tata Steel—among the biggest and most forward-looking corporates in India at its time—it was an uphill task to break the prevailing mental blocks in the government. While the Tata Steel (then TISCO) possessed two IBM 1401 computers, the Tata Motors (then TELCO) had three of them in the same city. For our overall work load planning, these were very low-capability second-generation computers—each with 256KB main memory—absolutely laughably small at today's scale of things. There was hardly any system SW.

Since any expansion and updating plans of computers were then strictly regulated by the government, proposals were made out to expand the systems to at least one MB main memory. The proposal also included request for some utilities and compilers that the revised configuration could support. Since DoE was handling the entire approval procedure, we all thought my handling the matter would bring quick results, thanks to my previous camaraderie.

Reaching Delhi, I was not ready for the rude shock. The licence-permit *raj* would not permit the expansion as contemplated by us. With a great deal of persuasion (which to me was entirely uncalled for), the powers-that-be agreed to a 348KB main memory and not an iota beyond, for each 256KB system ! I returned to Jamshedpur, severely crest-fallen. The Tata authorities as well as my EDP colleagues were hugely disappointed. Nothing much could be planned in advance with this kind of configuration, And about the systems software, the less said, would be better.

× × ×

In the northern part of Jamshedpur near Subarnarekha river was located the Xavier Labour Relations Institute (XLRI), the well-known centre of excellence, which conducted two 2-year programmes, namely, PGDBM (Post-Graduate Diploma in Business Management) and PGDIR (Post-Graduate Diploma in Industrial Relations). Within PGDBM, XLRI had introduced the course on "Production Planning and Control" (PPC) and was keen for academic inputs in their evening sessions, if it could be planned that way. Since I was just about handling the subject very much in practice, I was invited—for two successive academic years—to handle a full-semester course on PPC, planned as follows, with a heavy bias on computers:

- General principles and practices of PPC.
- Assembly-line production planning (as in the Tata Motors).
- Process-flow production planning (as in the Tata Steel).
- Instrumentation planning for assembly-line production.
- Ancillary development planning in process-flow production.
- Raw materials planning and control.
- Maintenance planning and control (e.g., Blast Furnace relining).
- Inventory planning and control.
- Production planning and scheduling (order-sequencing, to make production remain in step with a variable demand-profile).
- Product profitability planning.

- Rejection analysis.
- Use of Optimisation techniques in PPC.

It was great to interact with the Xaverians !

× × ×

Meanwhile, the National Committee on Science and Technology (NCST) under the Department of Science and Technology (DST), Government of India had set up in 1974, "NCST Panel on Futurology" in keeping with the trend in "Futures Study" all over the world. The concerns began with the Club of Rome studies that dramatically directed world attention to the implications of continued population growth, with hardly any diminution in that rate by 2000: from 4.0 billion in 1975 to 6.35 billion in 2000. While sectoral studies assumed that sufficient capital, energy, water and land would be available upto the millennium-end, integrated studies revealed their insufficiency in relation to the total population growth.

As proposed by XLRI, I took a brief course in 1977 on "Futures Study", covering *interalia* the following:

- Alvin Toffler's analysis, as in *Future Shock* (1970), giving the explosive changes in businesses, sub-cultures, life-styles and human relationships;
- State of the world as seen under Alvin Toffler's *The Third Wave* (1980), on the emergence of agricultural, industrial and post-industrial civilisations;
- The series of seminal reports submitted to the Club of Rome—a body concerned with the holistic well-being of mankind and future-oriented in its thinking—as follows:
  1. *The Limits to Growth* (1972), by Dennis Meadows (denouncing the growth obsession of a society in which every individual, family, group, corporation, or nation was trying to become bigger, richer and more powerful all the time);
  2. *Mankind at the Turning Point* (1974), by Mihajlo Mesarovic and Eduard Petel (an analytical tool for the present generation to assess their policies and strategies);
  3. *RIO: Reshaping the International Order* (1976), by the 1969 economics Nobel-laureate Jan Tinburgen (a meticulous

analysis of principles and measures needed for more just and equitable society for the poor and the deprived);

4. *Beyond the Age of Waste* (1978), by Dennis Gabor, *et al.* (on options to use science and technology wisely and well for moving to a higher plane of civilisation); and
5. *Goals for Mankind—on New Horizons of Global Community* (1977), by Ervin Laszlo, *et al.* (with attention on human element, especially differing cultural attitudes and value-theories).

- Inputs from the prestigious Hudson Institute—suggesting the contrary viewpoint that economic growth would continue well into the next millennium and reach an eventual world-wide plateau, characterised by affluence and universal high standard of living —
  1. *The Year 2000: A Framework for Speculation* (1967), by Herman Kahn, *et al.* and
  2. *The Next 200 Years: A Scenario for America and the World* (1976), by Herman Kahn, *et al.*
- Conclusions of these studies in each of the current problem areas—population, energy, mineral resources, food and environment. [For instance, the world's forests were now disappearing at the alarming rate of 18-20 million hectares a year with most of the loss occurring in the humid tropical forests of Africa, Asia and South America, vide *North-South: A Programme for Survival* (1980), prepared under the German Chancellor Willy Brandt.]

× × ×

In the prevailing atmosphere of systems thinking, mentioned above, XLRI graciously threw open to me part-time research facility—with full infrastructure provided. I took advantage of looking into some facets of social organisations: systems which contained purposeful parts with different roles and functions, and which were themselves parts of larger purposeful systems. In the four studies I was able to conduct—on *communications framework*; *indicators for quality of life*; *management of technology*; and *cybernetic approach to management planning*—focus was kept on three fundamental aspects: how to *design* and *manage* systems so that they could effectively serve their own purposes; what would be the purposes of their parts; and what would be the purposes of the large systems of which they were part. These were, in fact, the self-control, the humanisation and the environmentalisation problems respectively, according to Ackoff. The four studies are summarised below:

Communication framework—While "futures study" in the West, as seen above, had veered round sophisticated technology and gone towards new horizons of "experience" and "mosaic culture",—such studies in India had moved along different lines towards appropriate technology, participative society and community activity at grass-root levels. Keeping in view such handicaps as large population, lowlife-expectancy; mounting unemployment, malnutrition, inadequate water supply, lack of transport and a hybrid management culture,—there could be a long-term thinking on communication scenario, especially on the role of "variety" in human and social environment, communication service and communicator.

In a communication framework, the problem of variety had to be examined from both quantitative and qualitative angles. "Variety-matching" between the communicator and the communication service could try to achieve a balanced aim at social mobilisation. Some applications could be looked at from the viewpoints of "one-to-one", "many-to-one", "many-to-many" and "one-to-many" communication schemes. The need of monitoring information for mobilisation could also be emphasised.

Indicators for quality of life—Our concern was with futuristic thinking which could bring out the richness in visions among people, thus gaining richer images of future Indian society and aspirations for of Indian people. The "quality of life" of such a society should not only remain concerned with physical well-being of its individual members, but also satisfy their minimum welfare needs, and reach out to take on their human and societal development.

Construction of "perspective" indicators was recommended which would establish social goals, keeping in view an Indian *weltanschauung* (world-view), followed by "positional" indicators to measure the social conditions and changes taking place. The two could then be combined to derive "performance" indicators: for ascertaining improvement in the conditions of human existence with information on "quality of life" and for predicting future social events. An example was given of "positional" indicators for education, considering various factors and a comprehensive model was developed which could be based on quantitative observations and could assess changes in educational aspects of social life and social policy from present to future.

Management of technology—Technology, comprising human activities from agriculture to satellite communication, was defined as mass and energy transfer: involved in biological, chemical or physical form in order to produce the necessary change. While its technique had HW and SW contents, its structure had economic, social, cultural and cognitive aspects. In that way, technology corresponded to chromosomes carrying genetic codes. There was a dynamic relationship between society and technology, playing an important role in shaping technology: beginning from agricultural society up to the post-industrial society.

In practice, Indian technology scene had a most remarkable mix. Bio-technology was primarily concerned with agriculture and health-care, whereas hydro-technology was concerned with water management; and energy technology with coal-based, hydroelectric-based, nuclear-based and wind-based. Similarly, there were space technology and communication technology. Appropriate technology could be considered both from technology competence and technology self-reliance points of view.

Technology grew in the West based on "time-sharing" of knowledge; "space-sharing" of tools; and "group-sharing" of structured benefits. A study of time-interval between some inventions and their first commercial use in the UK led to the inference that capital-flow from India to England contributed to a cluster of inventions to be exploited. Analytical process in technology assessment was found important for determining sources of technology in government, namely, DGTD, CSIR, NRDC and DST.

Technology transfer could be of a *vertical* nature (i.e., from a donor organisation to recipient organisation) or of a *horizontal* nature (i.e., sharing of technology among different organisations or among developing countries). A systems approach to *international* transfer model could be developed with systems input, systems throughput and systems output vectors and illustrated for advanced computer technology. Similarly, a *national* transfer model could be developed illustrating lab-to-industry and lab-to-land schemes. Cost-benefit approach was recommended for alternative technology choices, where the rate of adoption depended on relative advantages, compatibility, complexity and other factors.

Cybernetic approach to sectoral management planning—It was early realised that cybernetic principles, as follows, applied to a large number of natural sectors:

- Short-cycled information feed-back and elimination of uncertainty;
- Choice of a set of critical variables;
- Achievement of ultra-stability through a fast feed-back loop which carried simple environmental inputs, perceived the process and adjusted the pre-programmed behaviour according to the inputs; and
- Monitoring of the critical variables and their changes through a second feed-back loop, producing major changes of state.

In India, industry sector was pretty well-organised in introducing computer aid in the following situations:

1. *Process control* where a high-degree of instrumentation was possible, and
2. *Operator guidance system* where high-degree of instrumentation was not feasible.

For instance, the following computer-aided systems could be noted for industry:

- *On-line process control system* (data through sensors, on-line data processing, on-line feed-back control, short response time);
- *On-line management control system* (data through manual terminals, on-line data processing, off-line feed-back for operator guidance, medium response time); and
- *Off-line management planning system* (Manual data, off-line data processing, off-line feed-back of control information for planning, long response time).

Agriculture sector, on the contrary, was the most disorganised, where a number of special programmes were introduced over time, covering some 2,000 blocks and planning to cover the remaining 3,000 blocks (out of a total of 5,000) phased over the next 10 years under

Intensive Rural Development (IRD). It was visualised that computer-aided data-base at district levels could help in:

1. *IRD Schemes* by combining area approach of projects with individual approach for *Antyodaya* schemes, and by monitoring physical performance against targets: block-wise and project-wise;
2. *Rural Credit Schemes*, operated through lead-bank concept of commercial banks; cooperation assistance for short-term loans; and agriculture development banks in the cooperative sector for medium-term and long-term loans; and
3. *Rural Industry Schemes*, for which district industry centres (DICs) were being set up to provide all infrastructural inputs, by maintaining adequate data-base and suggesting suitable action for decision-making in disbursing loans, blueprints for setting up industry and so on.

In energy sector, consumption had grown at the rate of nearly 7 per cent over the past 15 years, whereas annual economic growth rate was only 3.5 per cent. The energy control centres at Trombay, run by Tata Electric Company, had implemented liaison operation in automatic mode using PRODAC 50 and DEC/PDP 11/40 computers since the early seventies. It was possible to organise energy control centres around power grids, such as, State Grid; Regional Grid; and National Grid.

In refinery sector, one could use on-line automated sensors for gaseous stream to record gas-flow, pressure, temperature and level periodically and use these parameters to determine which fraction of each stream should be blended subject to constraints. The benefits of such feed-back control would be through savings on expensive components, reduction in wastage, improvement and consistency in product quality; flexibility in product-mix; and ultimately improved profitability.

In the water resource sector, it was possible to have a computer based operator guidance system to economise the resources. For instance, a model for operations at Nagarjuna Sagar reservoir—ensuring that peak-flood at Vijaywada at the downstream was within the safe limits of about one million cusecs—could take into account the following factors:

- Weather forecasts for various zones in the catchments area;
- The run-off observed at specified higher gauging stations;
- The flood-absorbing capacity of the upper reservoirs;
- The full reservoir (or any lower) level, varying between the lowest at the monsoon-beginning and the highest in November;
- Water-demand at various periods for irrigation and power generation; and
- Economic benefits arising out of water-release for these purposes.

Livestock sector (of cows and buffaloes) fell into two grades: essential and non-essential. While the essential livestock was to be nurtured and improved by cross-breeding, the non-essential livestock needed elimination to plug a huge annual wastage. Management planning for a rational livestock policy needed an appropriate information feed-back system.

Indian Railways sector were already planning to go for comprehensive computerisation, with large computer system at the Railway Board and at each of the nine zonal headquarters. It was possible to visualise a network of computers connecting all these, first, on off-line mode; later, making them on-line as communication improved. There were plans for on-line passenger reservation (IMPRESS) system, and on-line wagon movement and freight control system: the latter to regulate wagon traffic in different zones.

In health sector, the diseases were either water-borne (diarrhoea, cholera, etc.) or vector-borne (TB, malaria, etc.). There was no traditional system on measuring health statistics (morbidity and mortality) on a continued basis, in contrast to, say, collection of agricultural records through a *Patwari* system. Community health schemes, for planning purpose, could comprise :

1. *Permanent Data*—Household data, community health profile (indicators against standards), age profile (mortality at different ages), etc.; and
2. *Current Data*—Incidence of diseases, state of environment, pollution level, hygienic status, etc.

With the aid of decision-rules of health care and allocation pattern of health resources, one could visualise a computer-aided monitoring and control system for operating community health schemes.

In education sector, computers were so far used in the domains of examination result processing, entrance or selection tests and, in rare cases, university information system for budgeting and financial accounting. These apart, possibilities remained for developing personnel information system on teaching faculty and time-table system for allocation of faculty resources. Over and above these data processing applications, there could be innovative ways of creating decision-support systems by capturing data on social, economic and educational backgrounds of the student community. These could be supplemented by data on student-performance *vis-à-vis* socio-economic status of the students, namely,

- Geographical distribution within a State;
- Level of parental income groups;
- Social groups (religion, caste and community);
- Parental education groups;
- Environment (urban, semi-urban, rural);
- Medium of education; and
- Categories of schools (residential, missionary), etc.

The information, of both permanent and current type, could then be used to identify needs for :

1. Facility planning for students (hostel, health, etc.);
2. Faculty planning (for teaching staff);
3. Facility planning (for libraries, laboratories and courses); and
4. Financial assistance planning for the disadvantaged student community.

Lastly, in banking sector, development placed a high priority on social obligation of Indian banks operating loans and advances at differential rates of interest (4½ % or so) for the weaker sections of the community Dispensing with securities substantially and lending to "socially accepted business" made enquiries into credit-worthiness very necessary before giving bank-loans. Such enquiries could comprise:

- Survey of skills and training;
- Assessment of trustworthiness;
- Investigation on business status;
- Insistence on maintenance of accounts;

- Probe into financial statement for past three years;
- Survey of market competitions and employment potential;
- Satisfaction on past performance;
- Availability of personal guarantee; and
- Need for further counselling (at bank's cost) on how to conduct business.

The above one-time data-base could help fix a repayment programme and would need continuous supervision over a borrower's operation, such as :

- A client's business and the debits/credits to his accounts;
- Inspection of the client's books;
- Performance on sales, credits and creditors;
- Outside borrowings and order-book position;
- Monthly stock-statements on stock of finished goods and raw material;
- Semi-finished and finished production (for industrial concerns); and
- Annual profit and loss statements.

× × ×

The above applications were in the areas of *industrial cybernetics, rural cybernetics, energy cybernetics, resource cybernetics* and *social cybernetics*. They attempted in 1975-78, a pioneering approach to apply cybernetics—aided with computers and modern communication—to a number of important sectors of socio-economic development. The illustrations culled were in the nature of conceptual exercises,—all within the range of being feasible in practice, and could be multiplied manifold !

They were fascinating exercises for me, ensconced at the XLRI.

5

IT Crystallised (1978-80)

Vestiges of "licence *raj*" on import was still looming large on the horizon when I switched over as Director (Computer Division), Administrative Staff College of India (ASCI), Hyderabad in mid-1978, finding my place in the Court of Governors of ASCI along with three other Directors, beside the Principal. ASCI was a premiere body on management research, management education, management consultancy and computer services. A few other professionals from the Management Services of the Tata Steel joined ASCI along with me and it felt like home in the middle of a thoroughly professional milieu. [Such drastic changes in the job situation were a new phenomenon beginning to happen in the nascent IT market. The latter was thoroughly demand-driven where the few qualified professionals were chased by their overwhelming demand in the available IT HW and SW market and, quite often, the pay-packet rose every time a change in job was sought!]

Winds of change had begun blowing by then. One of the major forums for catalysing change was the Computer Society of India (CSI) from whose platform fellow professionals were voicing their strong reservations and airing dissent against the restrictions and regulations that prevailed in the land. CSI was a unique forum which provided umbrella to HW and SW engineers, teachers and trainers, and—most important of all—to the vast breed of computer end-users that was growing by the day in industry, business, administration and socio-economic vocations. CSI was the common meeting ground: with vendors, developers, manufacturers and service-providers, not to talk about the government officials and policy-makers.

I distinctly recall an instance of change where computer professionals, using CSI as their forum, played a catalytic role. This was when in 1976-77, government sought to alter IBM's near-monopoly role for supply of hardware and software in the Indian market and, in resentful protest, IBM planned to leave India. Since the IBM machines were offered to their erstwhile lease-holders at a throw-away price, the machines were consequently all retained. There was a hue and cry from the end-users, from the CSI platform, on how to continue maintenance of these fairly old machines and, almost in response, the government formed a public-sector unit, Computer Maintenance Corporation (CMC), with the primary role of maintenance of computers, especially the IBM ones. CMC and a private sector unit, International Data Management (IDM)—with a senior ex-IBM technocrat, Dr. OP Mehra, as its Managing Director—conveniently manned by former IBM engineers who took over the maintenance activity of all IBM machines virtually overnight. [Later on, CMC extended its functions—under the able leadership of Dr. P.P. Gupta—to all computer-related activities for a "single-point support" and thereby expanded a lot of activities all over the land: with its original charter of computer maintenance virtually played down, but that was another story.]

Almost in the wake of forming CMC, the wind of change had swept India to much further terrains, and a firm industrial and technology policy emerged from the government for minicomputers and microprocessor-based systems. Here is a flavour given *ad seriatim.*

× × ×

By mid-1979, DoE recognised that IT revolution had started growing fast, and that minicomputer and microprocessor-based systems could bring significant cost reductions, design simplifications and better flexibility in industry,—apart from finding a wide range of applications in several other areas of the economy. The government, therefore, decided that the minicomputer and microprocessor industry would be developed,—based on capability, size and structure of the system as well as type of application according to the following usage-categories:

- *Dedicated Applications*—Original Equipment Manufacturing (OEM) options for specific functions on a real-time basis, with nominal peripherals;
- *Standard On-line Applications*—OEM option with peripheral and SW;
- *Major On-line Applications*; and
- *Stand-alone systems*.

(1) Major objectives in the development of mini-computer and microprocessor industry would be to set up systems engineering companies which are not necessarily engaged in the manufacture of central processing units (CPUs) or peripherals. Manufacturers of processors and peripherals would also be permitted to produce minicomputer systems.

(2) For dedicated applications (like direct-data entry, invoicing machines, data-acquisition systems) and dedicated controllers,—medium and small-scale entrepreneurs with technical background would be preferred. For requirement of on-line and stand-alone applications, units from the organised sector would be considered. Qualified individuals and groups abroad wishing to return and invest in minicomputer-related industrial programmes would be actively promoted.

(3) A detailed scrutiny would be undertaken to ensure that the application areas in which the minicomputer/microprocessor system was to be used were in tune with national priorities. The industrial licensing policy would also continue to be restrictive in area where labour displacement was likely to be involved.

(4) Foreign technical collaboration for high-performance peripherals would be permitted on a selective basis. Only where sophisticated electronics was demonstrably in the interest of quality and development in the country, foreign technical collaboration would be permitted. Foreign brand names would be permitted for the explicit purpose of promotion of export sales.

(5) To facilitate programmes for systems engineering of mini-computers, industrial capacity for production of a standardised range of peripherals and CPUs would be built

up on an OEM basis, so that there was free indigenous availability of reasonably-priced building blocks for minicomputer and microprocessor-based systems.

(6) Until indigenously produced peripherals and CPUs were available, efforts would be made to import preferred components, CPUs and peripherals on a stock-and-sale basis to obtain price advantages.

(7) Performance of the units licensed and approved to make minicomputers and microprocessor-based systems would be reviewed annually and expansion of capacity approved on the basis of such review.

(8) All pending applications would be scrutinised with regard to viability of R&D facilities; capability to maintain standards and quality; current infrastructure and future potential.

An interesting offer was made by the government to use Indian languages on computers. To make such usage, appropriate input and output units were needed by way of HW and additional SW was to be developed for coding, text processing, translation and programming. Electronics Corporation of India Limited (ECIL) made preliminary efforts in using Indian languages on computers and succeeded in generating Devnagari and Telugu characters on display screen. They also developed a FORTRAN compiler to process texts in Hindi and Telugu. Concurrently, feasibility and potential of using Indian languages on computers were successfully taken up in the C-DAC, Pune, under the Generalised Information System Text-processing (GIST) for all major Indian languages under their brilliant research scientist Mohan Tambe.

× × ×

The Computer Division, ASCI, had found a unique way of going round the government's restrictive policy on import of large computer systems. At ASCI, we had established collaboration with the friendly nation of Soviet Union and procured from their official electronics body ELECTRONOG-TECHNICA (in short, ELORG) two advanced REYAD systems, namely, REYAD EC-1022 and EC-1032—by offering to develop sophisticated application and system software on a time-bound basis. Even that early, it was evident that India had the SW skills which could be put to use in such innovative manner. ELORG found it convenient to offer,, on sale, ASCI-generated SW to other countries in the Soviet bloc who were using REYAD systems. It was, therefore, a "win-win" situation for both ASCI and ELORG.

ASCI's Computer Division had the following functional groups:

— ***Software Development Group*** (for manufacturers):
This was organised with high-skilled professionals to cater to ELORG as follows:
- *Mathematical Programing System (MPS)*—For solving linear programing problems in the domain of OR; and
- *Compiler Construction and Optimisation*—Using the Assembly Language of the REYAD system, which was a painstaking operation. [Writing of compilers using standards of 'C' language came in vogue much later.]

The other packages, under consideration (during my trip to ELORG headquarters in Moscow in the end of 1978) were:

- *Mathematical Programing System Extended (MPSX)*—For extending MPS to mixed integer programing problems; and
- Vehicle Scheduling Package (VSP)—Dealing with operation of vehicles, their scheduling, route allocation and load distribution.

— ***Systems Consultancy Group*** (for commercial applications in the corporate market):
These were generally in the nature of data-processing applications—for earning ASCI's bread and butter!—varied from time to time, but included the following on a stable basis:
- Annual examination result processing for AP Secondary Board of Education, involving a very large number of secondary candidates—institution-wise, candidate-wise, subject-wise tabulation and documentation, upto mark-sheet stage.
[The above data-processing system had an eminent scope of being made into a decision support system for AP's socio-economic milieu. If the routine result-processing data could be added to the parental income, parental

education, parental caste and parental habitat data, these could be interrelated on-line to reveal socio-economic correlations of far-reaching consequence and used to make out a "decision-support system" on disbursement of stipends/scholarships; opening of special coaching classes; and offer of caste-based academic/financial assistance schemes. The ideas, however, seemed to have no takers, being perhaps a little ahead of its time.]

- Monthly/bi-monthly/quarterly electricity billing and recovery system for AP State Electricity Board for distribution of power for business utilities and domestic consumers—station-wise, substation-wise and maintenance of recovery statements and arrears records.
[The above data-processing system of power-distribution data could be stretched to correlate with power-generation data and power-transmission data: substation-wise, station-wise and local area-wise. Since there were perceived "leakages" and "thefts" perpetually complained about, resulting into huge revenue loss,—these computer-generated correlations could pinpoint the quantum of financial loss, right to the substation level. Again, there seemed to be no takers for such a "decision-support system", owing presumably to many reasons, including political ones.]
- Periodic release of upstream water accumulation at Nagarjuna Sagar Dam on Krishna River in A.P.—for hydroelectric power generation (with a high water-head on the upstream side) through a potential-drop and for water-distribution through the east-bank and west-bank canals for irrigation purposes (with a low water-head on the upstream side) through the opening of eleven sluice-gates.
[The above was an "operator guidance system" to supply water-output for hydel generation and for canals to irrigating crops, based on their respective demands after manually calculating the water-input from the rains (through rain-gauges) *plus* water-input from the tributaries (like Tungabhadra River) *minus* evaporation loss *minus* seepage loss. Residual water was also to be left on the upstream-side for future release: to meet the

downstream river-system need beyond Srisailam Barrage. The mathematical model of "operator guidance system" here was inspired by the "automated control system" of the Arizona State, USA, on Colorado River Dam in the Rocky Mountains, where the water-release operations were automatically controlled after instrumentally sensing the entire water-input data on rains, seepage, evaporation, etc.]

— ***Computer Training and Education Group*** (for conducting computer courses, programmes and workshops at ASCI, corporate premises or designated venues):
This was also a large revenue-earning function for ASCI, conducted at the following levels:
- *Appreciation Level* for corporate executives and managers;
- *Executive Level* as EDP (Electronic Data Processing) administrators and managers;
- *Higher Professional Level* as system analysts;
- *Lower Professional Level* as programmers; and
- *Entry Level* as data entry operators and computer operators.

There was an interesting adjunct Certificate in Data Processing (CDP) test run in collaboration with M/s Data Processing Management Associate—an international organisation—with equal weightage under:

1. EDP equipment;
2. Computer programing and software systems;
3. EDP equipment; and
4. Quantitative methods.

CDP test programmes were also capable of expansion into specialised areas, such as:

- Operative software design and microprograming;
- Higher level language concepts and design;
- Industrial use of computers, e.g., process control;
- Data programing management;
- Computer auditing;

- Science and engineering applications programing;
- Computer-based MIS design; and
- Data communications.

× × ×

In a 1980 study—conducted by a group under Prof. R.K. Arora of IIT, Delhi, where I was member-rapporteur—it was noted that India had around 500 third-generation computers and another 60 or so cleared in 1979-80 for large computer systems,—apart from 100 microprocessors and business machines currently installed. The summary report was submitted in Delhi to the national workshop on "Curriculum in the Areas of Computer Science and Engineering" in April 1980, where it was felt that there was a national need of the following kind of education programmes:

1. Bachelor of Computer Applications (BCA) with two years at Graduate level for computer programers;
2. Master of Computer Applications (MCA) with two years at Post-Graduate level for training system analysts.

The minimum educational background for BCA was recommended to be BA or BSc or BCom. This was to enable the graduate population to avail of the employment opportunity as programers, after obtaining BCA as a technical degree like BEd or BT. Similarly, the minimum educational qualification for MCA was recommended to be at a higher level, namely, BE or BTech, or, MSc or BCA. This was to enable acquisition of the higher skill of systems analyst within a spell of two years.

Our study identified the following institutions as suitable for imparting BCA:

- All engineering colleges;
- All regional engineering colleges (about 18);
- All universities with adequate facilities (about 50); and
- All regional computer centres (about 5).

Similarly, the following institutions were identified in the study as suitable for training in MCA:

- Indian Institutes of Technology (5);

- Indian Statistical Institutes (3); and
- Jawaharlal Nehru University, New Delhi.

[It was hugely gratifying to observe today that, with the growth of India-wide IT revolution, the degrees of BCA and MCA have come to stay as highly covetable qualifications; the number of institutions training for them has literally grown a thousand-fold; and the faith underlying our study-group's and the national workshop's findings have been vindicated many times over!]

— ***Computer Maintenance Group*** (involving preventive maintenance performed at regular intervals; corrective maintenance performed when the system fails; and on-line maintenance with self-contained diagnostic tests stored in the system-memory):
The most important factor in maintenance was found to be the "mean time to repair" (MTTR). The idea, therefore, was to minimise MTTR, comprising :
1. Time to organise maintenance personnel, tools, test equipment, etc.;
2. Time to diagnose;
3. Time to access the faulty item;
4. Time to replace or repair; and
5. Time to inspect and verify.

— ***Computer Operations Group*** (involving computer operation, data preparation, I/O scheduling, production/ quality control and A/C plant):
These were mostly routine functions.

× × ×

At ASCI, we noticed early that the EDP professional was a problem-solver of the highest order and his sensitivity to the job environment made him particularly vulnerable to the turnover problem. In order to keep the turnover to the minimum, it was imperative to provide professionals with satisfying jobs within the organisation. Strictly hierarchical jobs—in a chain of command and control, as prevalent in a production organisation or in defence hierarchy—were hardly recommended. Instead, "participative management", as advocated by the American organisational psychologist, Rensis Likert (1912-1981), was considered more suitable to EDP, in a two-pronged approach:

- There would be flexible teams, each with its own project leader and project members. The composition of the team would be valid only during the tenure of the project; and
- Participation could be part of different teams concurrently; thus, one professional could be leader of one project and simultaneously member of another.

We took the initiative to introduce new responsibility levels—for professionals from among our four normal functional groups—into six "participative" groups. The designations and individual salaries were kept unchanged and professionals could be members of more than one group, depending on their aptitude, organisational need and availability at a given time. The groups created a flexible process with double or triple involvements for each professional, out of free will. The "participative" groups—operating over a limited period with great success—were as follows :

— ***Marketing Promotion Group:*** It is responsible for creating and propagating awareness of computer services in the Indian management scene. The group printed and widely circulated brochures on "Computers in Public Systems". "Computers in Government", "Computers in Industry" and "Management Game with Computer Aid",—making further contacts for actually introducing computer services.

— ***Finance & Audit Group:*** It is responsible for project costing and watching performance against plans for individual projects. Realistic estimations were used to work out costs of new EDP projects, besides annual budget and its periodic updating.

— ***Internal Training Group:*** It is responsible for planning and conducting the training of professionals within the division so as to help them in self-development and career advancement. Besides comprehensive survey of qualifications and on-job experience of all computer professionals within ASCI, review was done on frontier areas of knowledge that would be useful and suitably implemented, if necessary, through training from IIM Ahmedabad, TIFR Mumbai, etc.

— *Systems Software Group:* It is responsible for providing systems programing support to the computer centre. The group took up system generation work for disk-based operating system (DOS) for handling multiple functions and assisted in making video display unit (VDU) terminals operational.
— *Hardware Consultancy Group:* It is responsible for widening the professional horizon of the system engineers whose main task had remained maintenance of the computer hardware. The group was asked to look for small-time jobs with computer hardware, where their experience and expertise could be of relevance. Contacts were established with CMC and Electronics Corporation of India (ECIL) for taking up testing and evaluation activities of computer peripherals.
— *Programme Operation Group:* Responsible for providing support to application programers using computer services. The group arranged to obtain the programme and maintenance manuals from the concerned systems analysts and programers and implemented them for production purposes. The group also provided voluntary programing support to outside clients in order to earn goodwill for ASCI.

× × ×

In the nascent days when IT revolution was just brewing and many user organisations (large and medium industry, public administration, business houses and public utilities) were setting up their computer centres starting from scratch, one general course that proved vastly popular at ASCI—and also with the large conglomerates like NTPC (at their training complex of Power management Institute)—was on "Computer Management and Planning". This course was built on our ASCI experience in the following lines:

1. *Computer Management* —
   (1) Organisation of computer centre,
   (2) Computer staffing and task-setting,
   (3) Personnel management for computers,
   (4) Cost management for computers,
   (5) Computer education and training, and
   (6) Computer and line management.

2. *Computer Planning* —
   (1) Selection and evaluation of computer,
   (2) Computer performance,
   (3) Planning for computer-I (large system in industry),
   (4) Planning for computer-II (mini system in industry),
   (5) Planning for computer-III (mini system in public administration),
   (6) Planning for computer-IV (microcomputer in industry),
   (7) Planning for computer-V (super-microcomputer in industry),
   (8) Computer maintenance.
3. Computer Frontiers —
   (1) Computer security,
   (2) Computer systems standards and systems audit, and
   (3) Computer ethics.

Another management-friendly training device was the running—by a set of competitive business-teams chosen from within the same firm—of specific business-activities that would begin from a given set of standard parameters and then would be simulated from year to year under varied circumstances, so that over a cycle of years, performance-results could be compared among the rival participating groups and winners decided among them. This was how a classic "business game" was run. The ASCI innovation was to inject a large array of decision-points at each simulated year-beginning and to furnish a set of computer-based algorithms to run them on-line and to arrive at quick outputs at the simulated year-end.

This was "Management game with computer aid",—for playing which corporate members of business houses (like the German Computer-peripheral firm BASF) would descend at ASCI; would spend 3-4 days with teams segregated from each other; would accept the given decision-inputs from my ASCI colleagues (like Dr. Kranti Amar who was the architect of many such "management games"); and arrive, at the end of the given simulated years, the business-outcomes for each "rival" team in order to decide on the winners. The element of fierce competition—in the middle of social bonhomie and camaraderie—was to be seen to be believed. Many enlightened firms (like BASF) evidently accepted our "Management game with computer aid": as learning tools to run and manage realistically their business enterprise-operations over the simulated period.

[A surprising amount of interest in "Management games with computer aid" was shown in the academic institutions in the USSR, UK, Poland and Hungary when I visited those countries later on. I think there has been enough untapped potential in this genre of management-learning still.]

× × ×

While Indian IT revolution was spreading—if not like wild, forest fire—like bush fire at the least, and while ASCI's Computer Division was playing a very positive role, the internal story was not entirely very rosy. ASCI's apex body, the Court of Governors, was not entirely supportive and, in a way, reflected the country's majority corporate scene. Mr. Dharma Vira, former Cabinet Secretary, chaired the Court, while Mr. Thomas, Chairman, Hindustan Lever, Mr. Prakash Tandon, former Chairman, Punjab National Bank and State Trading Corporation, and Directors of other divisions were its members: all fairly apprehensive of computer's labour-killing role. Although Mr. F.C. Kohli, Director-in-Charge, Tata Consultancy Service (TCS) and Prof. M.G.K. Menon, Chairman, Electronics Commissions, were also members of the Court, the prevailing opinion in the latter was decidedly against India's computerisation. It was a pity.

One of the causes of an anti-computer climate in the top corporate world was the lack of knowledge in the public domain. Mass media interest had not grown and Rajiv Gandhi's dynamic pro-technology and pro-computer role was still to appear: making all the difference. The *Hindu,* one of India's most serious journalistic ventures, had perceived this quite early. I got the idea when, during one of my Chennai trips (to attend the CSI Convention), I received an invitation to write regularly for the masses—on their Wednesday *Management* page—from Mr. N. Kasturi, the *Hindu* editor. Over a cup of percolator coffee, he asked me a startling question: "Which computer journals will you consult, while writing for us?" I responded by honestly naming the two I did get to see: *Dataworld* of the USA and *Computer Weekly* of the UK,—in the absence of any Indian journal yet to appear. Mr. Kasturi seemed to be satisfied and I was impressed by his journalistic integrity. Our collaboration began without further hitch.

For the next year and a half, the *Hindu* Wednesday page would almost unfailingly carry my public-interest story on computers, while some also appeared in the *Economic Times* and *Business World.* A sampling would be as follows:

Basic Concepts —

1. Meaning of Computer Power.
2. Utility of Software Tools.
3. Selection of Computers.
4. Evaluation of Computers.
5. Import of Computers.
6. The World of Microprocessors.
7. Microprocessors and Industrial Process Control.
8. Quality Control by Micros.
9. Selection of Microprocessors.
10. Advent of Personal Computers.
11. Distributed Data Processing.
12. Data Communications.
13. Computer Networks.
14. Patterns of Information Management.
15. Effective Management Information System.
16. Emerging Trends in Management Information System.

Real-Life Applications —

17. Accounting Systems.
18. Materials Control.
19. Industrial Productivity.
20. Natural Resource Sector—Remote Sensing.
21. Agricultural Sector—Marketing for Agricultural Produce.
22. Education Sector.
23. Health Sector.
24. Banking Sector.
25. Railway Sector—Cost *versus* Benefit.
26. Steel Sector—Decision-making.
27. State Administration.
28. Law and Order.
29. Public Utilities.
30. Helping the Disabled.
31. Aids to the Arts.
32. Computer-aided Engineering.

Related Issues —

33. Transition Strategy from Manual to Computerised.
34. Marketing Aspects of Computer service.
35. Publicity Pattern in Computer marketing.
36. Computer, Employment and Automation.
37. User Education in Computers—District Level.
38. User Education in Computers—State Level.
39. Computer Export Strategy.
40. Current Status of Operations Research.
41. Role of Computer-aided Optimisation.

Almost the entire lot came out as books, in response to suggestions from the enlightened readers of the *Hindu*. I, too, was happy to fulfil a mass media role!

6
IT Spread-Eagled (1980-84)

I shifted gears in January 1980 to Delhi, where I always wanted to return. The first thing that all of us could do in the capital was to get a bird's eye view of the world's leading third- and fourth-generation computer systems that had begun operating in our land:

• IBM	4300, 303X, 370, 360 series
• AMDAHL	470 V/5, 470 V/5-II, V/6, 470 V/6-II, 470 V7, V8
• EC SERIES	REYAD EC- 1022, EC-1032, EC-1033, EC-1035, EC-1040, EC-1045, EC-1060
• CDC	OMEGA 480 VI, VII Series
• ITEL	AS/3*3, AS/3*4, AS/4, AS/4 MP
[Above models were fully plug-compatible with IBM systems]	
• CDC	CYBER 170 and 70 Series, STAR Series-6000, 7000
• DEC	Systems 10 and 20
• HONEYWELL	60 Series, 2000 Series
• NCR	8000 Series, Century Series
• BURROUGHS	800 Series, 3800, 6800, 7800 Series
• HEWLETT PACKARD	1000, 2000, 3000 Series
• UNIVAC	90 and 9000 Series, 1100 Series
• ICL	1900, 2000 Series
• SIEMENS	4000, 7000 Series
• DATA GENERAL	NOVA ECLIPSE 8 Series

• CRAY RESEARCH	CRAY I
• FUJITSU	FACOM 230 Series
• HITACHI	HITAC M Series
• NIPPON ELECTRONICS	P 300 Series
• PHILIPS	16 Series
• INTERDATA	7/32, 8/32 Series, 700, 800 Business Series

[Many of the models had IBM architecture.]

Indian computer manufacturers were also operating competitively as follows:

• ECIL, Hyderabad	TDC-12, TDC-312, TDC-316, TDC-332, SUPER-16, MICRO-32, etc.
• DCM Data Products, Delhi	Spectrum 1-7, Galaxy-11 and 21, Micro-1121, DUAL, etc.
• Processor System India, Bangaluru	PSI System made on order, 8- or 16-bit, MINI-32, etc.
• ORG, Baroda	ORG-2001, ORG-20, ORG-60, etc.
• NELCO, Mumbai	NELCO-5000, NELCO-8000
• ICIM, Mumbai	2904, S-101, BUSINESS PC, etc.
• UPTRON, Lucknow	S-850, S-1650, etc.

The computer scene in India in the eighties, therefore, seemed poised at a reasonably organised level. Certain clear-cut government policies had also been evolved that could be summarised *ad seriatim*.

Import Policy—Procurement made over the years resulted in some advantages, such as,

- Centralised tendering on a broad basis with 5-20 vendors;
- Due to competitive bidding, prices to end-users made more rationalized;
- Users having experts configure cost-effective systems;
- Contractual terms made available to all users on equitable basis.

Self-reliance in Maintenance of Imported Systems—Since more than 80 per cent of computer installations were of IBM or ICL origin, the setting up of the CMC for providing support of all imported systems enabled India to obtain most contemporary systems within 6 months to one year of their being introduced in the home country.

Self-Reliance: R&D in Computers—While major funding for R&D took place in government-sponsored organisations, such as, DAE, ISRO, DST, DRDO, etc., R&D activities also spread industrial units in the public and private sectors and in the scientific societies recognised by the DST.

Self-Reliance in Indigenous Industry—Licensing guidelines of mini and microprocessor systems issued in 1978 recognised a broad-based industry in India with participation from all sectors.

Self-Reliance in Computer Manpower—Prof. V Rajaraman's Committee of 1980 recommended expansion and institution of more B.Tech and M.Tech programmes, besides the 3-year MCA programme and other teachers' training programmes.

Computer Software Export—Since technology trends made HW costs in computer systems less than one quarter of the total system cost and since SW market of the world ran into billions of dollars, the government's promotional guidelines enabled import of computers for SW exports—as was the ASCI case—by Indian professionals: on the basis of export-obligation of 200 per cent of the system cost over a 5-year period.

Setting Up of Standards—In order to create consciousness towards standardisation, Indian Standards Institute laid standards for various products, such as, electronic calculators, business machines, data processing, etc.

Foreign Equity—Such activities as R&D in the manufacture of computers, sub-systems and components fell under the Foreign Exchange Regulations Act (FERA) in the category of high-technology activities to permit higher level of foreign equity participation.

Monopolies—The Monopolies Restricted Trade Practices (MRTP) Act governed the expansion of industrial activities of those organised companies who came under its provisions.

On the whole, the indigenous industry was essentially supported at the level of micro, mini and small systems. Imports were permitted only if the indigenous systems could not meet specific user requirements. It was a welcome development covering the following:

- Technology build-up as a selective process to enable rapid build-up of self-reliance;
- Selectivity of applications to mitigate social imbalance;
- Tax relief and higher depreciation for investments on computers and R&D;
- Encouragement to all sectors for participation in computers;
- Educational and training programmes for reorientation and development of appropriate computer skills;
- Adequate security measures and legal provisions;
- Standardisation towards improved maintainability and faster growth; and
- Development of data communications networks.

× × ×

In Delhi, I had joined Computronics India, a forward-looking all-India computer corporate, involved mainly in commercial activities. As Senior Executive Director—virtually at CEO's level—I enjoyed pro-actively helping the enlightened ownership in two of their initial propositions:

1. *Cooperation with European Union*—A large delegation from the European Union countries was visiting India in association with the Export Promotion Council of India in 1980 to explore how far possibilities existed to let software be developed in our country in lieu of importing large European computer systems,—on the paradigm of the Soviet initiative successfully tried out at the ASCI. With impressive symposia held and some one-to-one across-the-table discussions arranged, a lot of goodwill was generated for the systems from the continental Europe, which were seeking to compete for a foothold in the developing world against their American counterparts. Keeping in view the latter's well-known clout, not much of concrete outcome, was in evidence.

2. *Establishment of an Apex Institute for Software Education*—The Computronics management was keen in 1981 to set up a high-profile institution for software training and education for creating high-level, qualified manpower what the universities and other official academic bodies were unable to produce. It was a quite laudable idea and a preliminary meeting—to decide on strategy, modalities, teaching curriculum and recruiting faculty—was held in 1981. Prof. P.V.S. Rao of

the Tata Institute for Fundamental Research (TIFR) was invited to take a lead-role, along with Prof. R.K. Arora of IIT, Delhi. While considerable progress was made about the constitution of the proposed institution, the major bone of contention was the financial back-up. While the educationists proposed an independent body run by a charitable agency funded by Computronics, the management of the latter had the vision of a commercially-run Computronics Institute for Software Education. The latter view did not quite jell with the academicians and it seemed to be "an idea whose time has not yet come".

[Around the same time in 1981, NIIT—named grandiosely by a splinter group of HCL as "National Institute for Information Technology", but later abbreviated to its acronym "NIIT"—came into being and it made definitely a dent in the low-profile software manpower market in India. But this was not quite the same as the high-profile body visualised by the Computronics management, which never came in existence in the Indian private sector. Was there a learning lesson of the return-on-investment kind ?]

× × ×

Computronics kindly permitted me to make presentations on IT and OR in three significant international conferences: as sponsored by UNESCO in Dublin, Ireland; as sponsored by International Federation of Operations Societies (IFORS) in Hamburg, Germany; and as sponsored by International Federation of Information Processing (IFIP) in Jerusalem, (Israel).

In March 1981, UNESCO sponsored me for "Informatics and Industrial Development" held at the heritage-site of Trinity College, Dublin, where I presented two papers: "Control Informatics—Its Role in Developing Countries" and " Appropriate Informatics in Industry—A Third World Viewpoint". I also chaired the Workshop Session on "Computerisation in Different Industrial Sectors, Surveys and Case-Studies of Advanced Applications, Informatics and Small and Medium Scale Enterprises" [alongside the noted Prof. R. Narasimhan from India, chairing "National Policies for Development of the Informatics Industry and National Infrastructure for the Utilisation of Informatics"].

In "Control Informatics", I referred to the 1973 UN ACAST Working Group which recognised levels of computer usage as: basic, operational and advanced, placing India at operational level (with

Argentina and Mexico). To resolve an information gap between the "information rich" and "information poor" countries, I suggested strategies on informatics: "on-line transmission—developed to developing countries" and "on-line transmission among developing countries". Under the 1978 UN Conference on Technical Cooperation among Developing Countries, a development information network (DIN) was to design a two-way flow among national centres, regional centres and inter-regional centres. I commented upon transfer of technology from developed to developing countries, involving large data bases and feed-back information systems: within a developing country. I provided illustrations of control informatics in education, employment, health, food and housing.

In "Appropriate Informatics in Industry", I referred to the 1979 OECD study "Facing the Future", and developed the basic ideas of "Appropriate technology" as follows:

1. Automated control of industrial process to be tried only at operational level with its high degree of instrumentation;
2. Since decisions were not programed (although repetitive) at managerial level, automated computer control to be discarded in favour of operator guidance;
3. At the strategic control level, off-line computers to be justified for specific problem-solving.

I provided illustrations of operational control, managerial control (on-line and off-line in a batch-mode) and strategic control mainly from Tata Steel and Tata Motors.

While chairing the Workshop Session on "Computerisation in Different Industrial Sectors", I received forwarded interesting recommendations from the participant countries:

- Wide differences in characteristics;
- Divergence in structural and cultural constraints;
- Human factor as making the major limitation on the application rate of informatics;
- Limitations resulting from poor system design, lack of awareness, lack of dedication and coordination;
- Need of detailed comparative case-studies;
- Incremental forms of innovation and avoidance of sweeping changes;

- Need of sectoral studies to identify skill requirements;
- Emphasis required on managerial aspects of informatics;
- Need of sound information base to guide policy;
- Need of case studies to evaluate economic usefulness of data bases like ISIS;
- Evaluation of alternative ways of implementing computer applications;
- Under-utilisation of computers in production and process fields;
- Use of inexpensive microcomputers;
- Computer-aided design applications to facilitate manufacturers;
- Use of microprocessor-based devices in vehicles for energy-saving; and
- Development of standards by large organisations.

In July 1981, IFORS sponsored me—as I was then the national President of the Operational Research Society of India (ORSI)—to present a paper on "Operational Research and Government of India" in the international conference "Operational Research 81" in Hamburg. I divided the inter-disciplinary approach of OR into classical OR, technical OR and contextual OR. Applying OR to government implied a process of change, involving awareness; interest; evaluation; trial and adoption. In defence—traditionally the first—OR touched upon weapon systems; logistic systems; tactics and strategy; communication and control; inventory—for Air Force; weapon system, tactics and strategy, inventory—for Navy, with accent on reliability, queuing, mathematical modelling, searching, networking, etc. Indian P&T applied OR to solve inefficient queues in offices and inventory problems. Health applications of OR included classification and analysis of inventory of medicines, queues at hospitals under CARE, and growth and spread of malaria in AP villages. Indian Railways used OR extensively in inventory management, reservation systems, production for electric engines, capacity utilisation for diesel engines and use of shunting and train formations at marshalling yards. For Police force, OR studies covered optimal utilisation of policemen at different police stations and inventory management. In general, OR studies had been quite varied including levels of foodstock at warehouses; unloading of food-ships at seaports; and input-output approach for agricultural and industrial sectors. Sporadic use of OR needed, however, a concerted approach to socio-economic phenomena.

In May 1984, IFIP sponsored me to present a paper on "User Education in Informatics and Its Impact—An Indian Overview" in the IFIP WG3.4 Working Conference on "The Impact of Informatics on Vocational and Continuing Education" in Jerusalem. User education in informatics was far from organised in a developing country like India. I drew upon the experience in the engineering industry, process industry, defence production industry, Railway service, banking service and public administration—attempting an overview of the requirements, methodology and benefits of a systematic approach. I emphasised the significance of selection, basic sensitisation, detailed exposure and dovetailing of project/demonstration, and assessed the likely impact.

× × ×

While Computronics India continued its varied data processing activities and the ELORG's REYAD system liaison functions in Delhi, Mumbai, Allahabad, Lucknow, Kolkata and Kharagpur—in all of which I had an integral role—my major attraction for this organisation was its management's unequivocal support lent to the Computer Society of India (CSI) where I could play some useful roles.

From a modest 20 institutions and 35 individuals who constituted its membership during inception in Hyderabad in 1965, the CSI family grew to 750 institutions and nearly 10,000 individuals on its membership rolls, by the mid-1980s. By then, the CSI Regions (North, West, South, East) had elected Vice-Presidents and the CSI Divisions (Hardware, Software, Scientific Applications, Business Applications, Education, Data Security, Microcomputers) had elected Divisional Chairmen. As a member of the International Federation of Information Processing (IFIP)—with representation in all its technical activities—CSI's comprehensive computer activities in India were centred on its Chapters located at 30 townships and 13 branches for student members, all centrally coordinated.

CSI endeavoured to bring into focus problems of national importance through adoption of appropriate themes for its Annual Conventions and Exhibitions. Thus, issues such as Ideal Computer Image of India (1966); Computers in the University (1967); Computer

Education (1968); Training on Software (1969); Automation Problem (1970); Regional Centres (1971); Computers and Development (1975 and 1979); Manpower Development (1982); Productivity (1983); Communications (1984); Advancement of Rural Society (1985); and Productivity and Quality (1986) were projected and deliberated upon.

As CSI's Regional Vice-President for the northern region (1981-83), I had the opportunity of organising a regional conference in the salubrious weather of Dehra Dun in June 1982. Our theme was: "The State-of-the-Art of Computer Applications in India: Computer Modelling for Techno-Economic Development". The special feature of the conference was that the cases and applications were all obtained by inviting—mainly from the northern region—user-organisations and institutions themselves, and not by soliciting contributions from individuals without endorsement from the parent bodies (as was usually the case in conferences). We were given encomium for such a unique endeavour, since different organisations were presenting their actual experience and plans regarding computer applications in their own spheres.

The presentations covered the following :

National Development —

- *Computer in National Planning*—Planning Commission, Delhi.
- *Computer in Satellite Data Processing*—National Remote Sensing Agency, Secundrabad.
- *Computer in Environmental Modelling*—Indian Meteorological Department, Delhi.
- *Computer in Surveying and Mapping*—Survey of India, Dehra Dun.

Sectoral Development —

- *Computer in Agriculture*—Indian Agriculture Research Institute, Delhi.
- *Computer in Forestry*—Inspector General of Forests, Delhi and Forest Research Institute and College, Dehra Dun.
- *Software Development in Forest Survey*—Forest Survey of India, Dehra Dun.

- *Computer in Census Operations*—Registrar General of India, Delhi.
- *Computer in Maintenance and Personnel Management (Air Force)*—Air Headquarters, Delhi.
- *Computer in Personnel Management (Army)*—Army Headquarters, Delhi
- *Computer in Research and Development Management (Defence)*—Defence R & D Organisation, Delhi
- *Computer in Oil Exploration*—Oil & Natural Gas Commission, Dehra Dun

Technical Development —

- *Computer-aided design in engineering research*—Structural Engineering Research Centre, Roorkee.
- *Computer-aided design in engineering projects*—Engineers India, Delhi.
- *Application potential of LISP (a higher-level programing language)*—Jawaharlal Nehru University, Delhi.

Educational Development —

- *Computer-assisted Learning*—Technical Teachers' Training Institute, Chandigarh.
- *Computer-managed Instructions*—Technical Teachers' Training Institute, Bhopal.
- *Microcomputers in Education and Training*—JK Institute of Applied Physics & Technology, Allahabad.

One useful suggestion received was that CSI should be registered with the Indian Standards Institution (ISO), for creating a standards culture in the computer applications for techno-economic development.

× × ×

CSI held its Twentieth National Convention on "Computers for Advancement of Rural Society" in Delhi. Keeping in view the importance of the theme, it was decided to hold a two-day pre-convention National Workshop, in March 1985, in association with

DoE; Council for Advancement of Rural Technology (CART); IIT Kanpur; Indian Council for Medical Research (ICMR); and United Nations Educational, Social and Cultural Organisation (UNESCO): to define different thrust areas; elicit status reports on work known to have been done; and look at likely problem areas. [The national workshop became international by participation of Afghanistan and Nepal, thanks to UNESCO sponsorship.] I was privileged to be the Convener.

At the outset, it was illuminating to hear officially the Hon'ble Minister in-charge of Rural Development to pronounce: "So far computers have remained, by and large, an *urban phenomenon* (italics ours). Computers can be *rather dangerous* (italics ours) in an uncontrolled environment. Since it seeks to replace an established routinised pattern of implementation, reporting and management control, one has to practise *extreme caution* (italics ours). A computerised management information system is *bound to affect* (italics ours) management practices and hierarchical relations in a significant manner". All this was in the year of our Lord 1985 !

Dr. N. Sheshagiri, DG of NIC, set the positive note by describing how a weather satellite picked up photographs of a disaster-prone cyclone developing over the Bay of Bengal; how it relayed the status information to a ground station; how the ground station analysed, on computer, the information for working out trends; and how it was possible to find out where the cyclone was likely to hit the coast. Accordingly, warning could be given to a number of villages in that zone and several thousands of lives were saved! He also outlined how it was planned to connect the regional NIC computers at Delhi, Pune, Chennai and Bhubaneshwar with district computers and with terminals at taluk at one end, and to the central NIC CYBER system at the other end—by using INSAT satellite.

Theme Reports—containing quintessence of deliberations of the eight thrust-areas, presented by subject-area experts with considerable track-records themselves, as follows:

- Micro-level planning — V.M. Sundaram
- Rural food and agriculture — C.C. Maji
- Rural education — R.K. Sachdeva
- Rural health — C.V. Satyavati and K. Satyanarayana

• Rural communication	Y.L. Agarwal and I.T. Vishwakarma
• Rural industry	A.C. Jain
• Rural banking and finance	Nalin Kohli and Satish Kumar
• Rural environment	R.K. Dutta

Status Reports—Presented by NIC professionals on a number of applications developed by them, as follows:

1. *Micro-Planning A District Level*—Micro-level industrial planning; micro-level monitoring of middle-class family living; micro-level monitoring of integrated development scheme and welfare scheme; micro-level planning for social consumption and construction activities.
2. *Rural Food and Agriculture*—Agricultural input-output monitoring system; agricultural farm management system; monitoring of integrated rural development programme.
3. *Rural Education*—Adult education programme; directory of colleges; statistics of education in India (formal and non-formal education).
4. *Rural Health*—National-level information base; directory of hospitals in India; analysis of all health-related research projects.
5. *Rural Industry*—Monitoring system of all letters of intent / industrial licences; monitoring system of foreign collaboration agreements; financial analysis of large-sized companies; directory of all joint-stock companies; production information system for public sector undertakings; monthly production data-base for selected 183 companies under DGTD.
6. *Rural Banking and Finance (Potential Projects)*—Integrated credit planning and monitoring; information system standardisation in banking practice and procedures; plan of training programmes.
7. *Rural Environment*—Supports for forest information system, environmental information system, integrated economical data-base; natural resource data management system.

It emerged clearly that computer applications for rural sector would be either *direct* kind (involving district and taluk computers with village terminals) or *indirect* kind (with rural information system for decision-making). Both kinds of applications would relate to social production, social consumption and valuable social service.

× × ×

An interesting aside during my stay with Computronics was my attendance at the IFIP World Conference in Adelaide (Australia) (and the return journey *via* Indonesia, Singapore and Sri Lanka, to liaise with their computer activities). While mine was an academic paper presentation at the IFIP, there was an official presentation on India's status of computers by the then Secretary of DoE. To my consternation—and to the amazement of everybody from India present there—the official presented as *fait accompli* an impressive array of activities which, as known to all of us, was a mere "wish-list". When, later, politely confronted by us, the worthy gentleman confessed that he "just bent it a little" to impress the world congregation. We from India only gasped at the sheer audacity of it all !

7

Government-IT Interface (1984-89)

By the late-1984, when I joined All-India Management Association (AIMA) as its Director General—initially named Chief Executive—the management-IT interface had reached its pinnacle in Indian Subcontinent. FC Kohli, Director-in-Charge, TCS, and a doyen of Indian IT, had done the prognostication on "Future of Computers" for our ASCI course on "Computer Management and Planning", most of which had come through by now. These forecasts were as follows:

On-line Computer Systems

Extending computers from real-time mode to :

1. Retrieving isolated data-items for monitoring,
2. *Ad hoc* analysis of data-files for ranking, determining risk-level, etc.,
3. Estimating consequences of proposed decisions, and
4. Making decisions.

Focussing on overall efficiency and flexibility:

1. Enquiry and information retrieval system,
2. On-line reservation system,
3. Order-entry system,
4. Receipt and issue system,

5. Production planning and scheduling system, and
6. Product design system.

Data-bases

At present, we had batch processing with data rigidly divided into separate files. From there, major business and government, and even engineering design applications would move on to data-bases and later on, to very large data bases. It would, however, take time to move on to distributed data bases.

Computer Networks

Networking would extend the reach of computers, and enhance reliability, quality and cost performance. Tying computers together in a network would make their power more accessible, reliable and economical, since each could access more applications. Computers and terminals could be granted access to data-bases throughout a network, job-tasks and information files: transferred from one point to another, with shared data-processing resources.

Distributed Data-bases

Distributed data-base management systems would be involved in strong relevant parts of data-bases at different sites in a distributed network. Several such systems would be established in computer networks, including medical information systems, airline reservation systems and the like.

Microprocessors

A large range of mini-microprocessor products were to be introduced, influencing the design of virtually all digital systems, such as :

1. Front-end communication processors,
2. Remote concentrators and multiplexers,
3. Maintenance processors,
4. Magnetic tape and disk controllers,
5. Nodal processors in a network,

6. I/O processors,
7. Intelligent terminals, and
8. Word-processing and office automation equipment.

Statistical Analysis and Forecasting

1. "What was likely to happen" type of questions falling into the category of forecasting, to predict future events, such as, size or quantity of future occurrence; trend predictions; lag-corrections;
2. Results of forcing functions, such as, seasonability, life-cycle, sales prediction, etc.; and
3. Step functions, such as, advertising to open new territories, expanding sales force, and so on.

Simulation and Modelling

These would be a "what-if" question-structure. Basic task of simulation was to provide a "laboratory" in which real-world systems could be explained and predicted without disturbing them, without destroying them and even before building them. The tool of simulation was heuristic modelling. With computers, we would be concerned with simulation models, optimisation models and mathematical models, using logical representation of problems.

Deterministic and Probabilistic Models

With either type, the user would adjust the variables under his control to search for the most promising plans among those proposed. They would find applications in diverse areas, such as, manufacturing, design, sales, organisation, corporate strategy and planning.

Optimisation Studies

"What was best" type of questions would lead to optimisation studies. Types of problems amenable to optimisation studies were:

1. Electric power distribution — Load dispatch,
2. Machine assignment—Lowest cost plan,
3. Production scheduling,

4. Transportation—Lowest cost plan,
5. Blending—Best mix of ingredients, and
6. Investment portfolio.

Most of Mr. Kohli's visions had come true by the mid-1980s.

× × ×

With an early graduateship in management from the BIM, UK, tucked under my belt and with a mind-set ripened with over a decade's exposure to IT as it was evolving in India, I joined AIMA in 1985 with high hopes. After all, this was the apex body created for promoting professional excellence in management—as a super NGO with over 50 local management associations (LMAs) affiliated to it. In turn, it was part of the management movement in the Asian continent under Asian Association of Management Organisations (AAMO), which, in turn, was a part of CIOS (World Council of Management). It was run by a Council elected annually from the Indian corporate world and was headed by a President eminent in management—rotated among North, South, East and West India.

A personal SWOT analysis for AIMA of my time revealed to me four features:

- **Strength** (S)—Very well-represented in business and industry;
- **Weakness** (W)—Little recognised in public administration and government;
- **Opportunity** (O)—AIMA could definitely use upcoming IT, enhance tie-ups with AAMO and CIOS, create a long-range vision for itself; and
- **Threat** (T)—AIMA should not be perpetually engulfed by fund-crunch, unable to acquire even much-needed extra office-space.

In order to overcome weakness and create opportunity, I opened parleys with Ministry of Education. My bonding with the Education Secretary, Anand Sarup, worked well and the first-ever National Workshop on "Management of Education" resulted in 1985—sponsored by the Ministry and crafted superbly by S.L. Rao, the then AIMA President.

The Workshop's huge success led to further bonding with the Ministry, which sanctioned a grant of Rs. 5.0 lakhs towards AIMA's computerisation: again a "first" to an NGO on that date. One thing led to another and I took Education Ministry's letter to Dr. N. Sheshagiri, DG, NIC, then under Planning Commission,—pleading that AIMA's comprehensive computerisation would provide philip to the country's business and industry, and would allow LMAs to fall in step. NIC willingly sanctioned a handsome grant of nearly 12.0 lakhs towards AIMA's computerisation.

Now it was my turn to organise IT for AIMA. We selected, from the market, the PSI Mini-32 computer as the best-fit for AIMA; negotiated a fair price from the PSI chief, Vinay Deshpande; recruited a competent IT professional to head a newly-created IT division; and organised air-conditioned space and infrastructure. Well begun was half done!

× × ×

"When Ministry of Education and Planning Commission were there, could the rest of the government be far behind?" In a sense, the administrative machinery just opened the doors, and this time it was with a novel purpose. Department of Personnel Training and Administrative Reforms were seized with a new directive from the powers-that-be. All IAS officers would have to undergo one-week "Refresher Course" thrice in their life-cycle: once in early career, second time in the mid-career and finally once in the end-career. S. Chandrasekhar, Joint Secretary, was the concerned official who was planning and soon enough, I could persuade him to put AIMA on that department's radar.

It was fascinating to watch—for the first time in AIMA's history—the nattily-dressed senior IAS officers trooping into the "Management House" lecture-theatre and undergoing, as participants, the rigours of fresh training for an entire week. It so happened that I was ordained to take, within the one-week programme, the complete IT module that I divided into eight sessions as follows :

- Introduction to HW;
- Introduction to SW;
- Selection and Evaluation of Computer systems;
- Selection and Evaluation of SW Packages and Products;
- Computer Applications in Business and Industry;

- Computer Applications in Central and State Administration;
- Computer Applications in Public Utilities (Railways, Airlines Banks);
- Overview of Emerging Technology (Networks, Communications, Security).

  [I hugely enjoyed the experience of lecturing to the civil service luminaries whom I personally met in the AIMA class room. They included, among others, Mr. Venkitaramanan, the Principal Finance Secretary—the senior-most IAS officer in the country—Mr. Bhaskar Ghosh, I&B Secretary, Mr. P.C. Hota, UPSC Chairman and a host of others. In fact, Mr. Hota recalled, when I chanced to meet him decades later that apparently I once returned from Chennai by a morning flight, went straight to the class to keep my tryst and, only in the mid-lecture, took the participants' leave to go to the wash-room for freshening up!]

That was not all. There were also government directives for IAS officers to go through one 4-week "Refresher Course" at any one point of time in one's whole career. All these programmes were zealously taken up by LBS National Academy of Administration (at Indra Bhavan campus), Mussoorie; and other IAS training and induction academies as in Nainital, Jaipur, Srinagar and Thiruvananthapuram. My AIMA reputation preceded me: to find myself repeatedly travelling to those academies and to take the computer modules. Nainital (under Mukul Sanwal) and Thruvananthapuram (under Padma Ramachandran) experiences were particularly rewarding for their directors' unbridled enthusiasm every time! [Between AIMA and those academies, I could count, at one point of time, having lectured to every one, out of three IAS officers, in the country!]

Other cadres followed. Foreign Service Institute (then at Akbar Bhavan campus), Delhi, for IFS officers and for foreign diplomat-congregations; Shimla (Yarrow campus) for IA&AS officers; and Internal Security Academy, Mt. Abu, for BSF/CRPF officers They all sought to teach IT—in one garb or the other—and I was always proud of my AIMA connection to have it snow-balled.

There was snow-balling of another kind—this time overseas. Commonwealth Secretariat, UK, was seized of the matter and was watching closely the Indian administrative experience in IT. It struck them that IT induction in governance could have an African resonance. Prof. Mohan Kaul (ex-IIM, Ahmedabad) was occupying an important position at Pall Mall in London; he came over to AIMA to discuss matters. The outcome was a pan-African conference at the East and South Africa Management Institute (ESAMI) in Arusha (Tanzania) (under the shadows of Mt. Kilimanjaro)—followed by one more at Kenyan Institute of Management (KIM) in Nairobi (Kenya)—to discuss and evolve an African strategy. It was interesting to remain involved and share the AIMA process with another continent.

Yet another kind of snow-balling, of inter-governmental kind, was what UNESCO sought to achieve among the regional countries in South Asia. At the grand initiative of Dr. Aram Akopov, Regional Representative of UNESCO, a series of cross-country discussions took place in the following regional cities:

- Kathmandu (Nepal) [where I prepared additionally a blue-print for "National Nepal Network" (NNN) for their 16-district computer-connectivity plan, following closely the NIC model in India, but also delineating the proposed distributed data-base system (DDBS). This was deliberated upon at an official Singha Darbar conference for adoption];
- Colombo, Sri Lanka [where we had a preliminary meeting before getting together in Male];
- Male (Maldives) [where we went to a picturesque resort island for a secluded 2-1/2 (two and a half days) regional conference on "Inducting IT in Governance", amidst charming surroundings];
- Kabul (Afghanistan) [where we had another regional conference on "Inducting IT in Governance", with an eye-opening tour of Kabul Museum, now totally demolished, and splendid hospitality from our Afghan hosts].

A huge benefit from the above association with UNESCO was their inspecting AIMA's own IT computer facilities, availability of qualified IT staff (including myself) and the overall credibility in conducting training and education programmes. Satisfied with our credentials, UNESCO designated, in 1988, AIMA as "UNESCO's Regional Centre for Distance Education to conduct programmes in Informatics and Management for South and Central Asian countries".

Coming from UNESCO, it was quite a feather in AIMA's cap!

× × ×

Two spin-offs came from the Government of India's tie-up with AIMA to train IAS officers from 1987 onwards, well into 1988. Out of the two, the first one nearly succeeded, the second one did not.

The first spin-off was that several IAS officers, having passed through the portals of AIMA, expressed a desire to remain in touch with AIMA and its management ethos. It struck me that the model of "special interest group" (SIG) that operated in CSI nationally and in IFIP internationally, could serve this purpose well. While the idea did not make much progress (as the "refresher courses" themselves petered out by 1989), a similar idea—management development programme (MDP) exclusively for women executives—caught root. Dr. Reena Ramachandran, ex-ONGC, vibed well to my idea of SIG and organised a very successful MDP in 1987, leading to her formation of a strong SIG group for women executives, later on.

The second spin-off was the government's realisation that the IAS officers themselves brought in an enormous wealth of experience and expertise in the "refresher courses" and contributed hugely to the enrichment of the class by way of feed-back. When I carried this viewpoint to the concerned Jt. Secretary, Mr. Chandrasekhar, the latter responded enthusiastically, proposing that we could collect—at AIMA and other training institutions—these experiences as valuable "case-studies" and eventually have them edited and published. For the same reason as above, the idea never materialised and the "case-studies", begun painstakingly to be collected were perhaps gathering dust somewhere in the "Management House".

× × ×

In May 1986, the Allahabad-based National Academy of Sciences, India, organised—in collaboration with DoE, Council of Scientific and Industrial research (CSIR), Department of Ocean Development and CMC Ltd.—a National Seminar on "Electronics for teaching and Mass Education" in Delhi. I was invited to present a paper on "Electronic Media for Mass Education". I suggested that the "technology-poor" countries of the South were by no means "culture-poor" ones, in the prevailing North-South dialogue. In the quest for developing economic self-reliance, the countries from the South faced a threat of advanced technology from the North: to swamp their cultural identity. The idea of not merely conserving a rich heritage of the performing arts and fine arts, but also letting them flourish and cater to the growing base of populace and variety of taste, should be our central concern. By leap-frogging into the modern micro-electronics means available at present, one could visualise—for the first time in our civilisation—the utility of electronic media: as a powerful aid to training and education, research and development, production and propagation, awareness and sensitisation. For the arts. I proposed that ARTWARE—a processed art product or material (inclusive of idea, theme, style or presentation) that could be collected, stored, transmitted and delivered—could fully utilise electronic media to bring the arts heritage to the teeming millions, as well as allowed to grow, through the following four steps :

1. **Education**—Teaching, learning and training in the arts;
2. **Innovation**—Further development of the arts through experimentation;
3. **Production**—Performance and propagation of the arts; and
4. **Sensitisation**—Awareness-creation among viewers in the arts.

Given India's rich environment of the arts, the electronic tools could help in developing concrete art programmes (ARTWARE) locally, nationally and regionally, if not globally.

× × ×

There was a post-script on the computer exposure to the IAS officers during the "refresher courses" that involved me on the IT module such a lot. Some authorities (like Mr. Dinesh Sharma, the author) criticised that the link between the politicians and technocrats that Rajiv Gandhi had presided over in 1985-89 (*vide* Chapter 9, "IT: Have Wings, Shall Fly!"), when he was in power, "faced a strong backlash from the IAS lobby, which finally saw the bureaucracy wrench back all the authority in the IT domain by 1990". Was it an entirely a fair statement? On the contrary, was not the so-called "IAS lobby" becoming computer-savvy also a factor for getting IT revolution and e-governance going on smoothly, as we take them so much for granted today ?

No. 1: 1951 UNIVAC Large

No. 2: 1984 Apple Machintosh

No. 3: Mini Computer

No. 4: Fifth Generation Computer

No. 5: CSIRAC 1950s Original

No. 6: ENIAC

No. 7: First Generation of Computers

No. 8: First Generation of Computers

Replacing a bad tube meant checking among ENIAC's 19,000 possibilities.

No. 9: First Generation of Computers

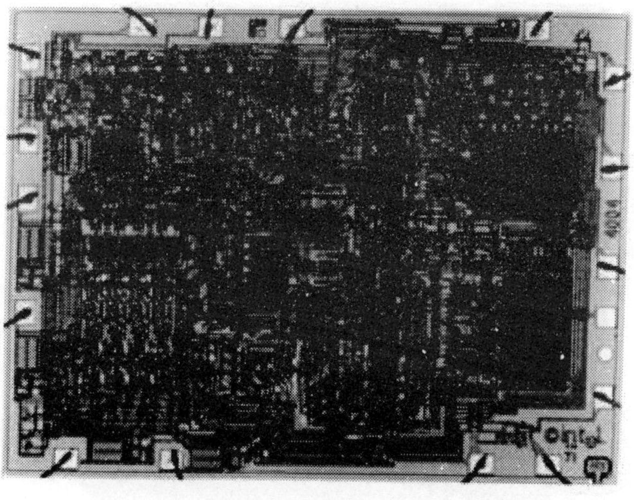

No. 10: Fourth Generation Microprocessor

No. 11: IBM 650 WEB

No. 12: Minecraft - 3DS

No. 13: EUERE PC

No. 14: Second Generation Computer

No. 15: Third Generation Computer

No. 16: UNIVAC

No. 17: UNIVAC Computer

No. 18: Vacuum Tubes First Generation

No. 19: Vonneumann

8

Industry-IT Interface (1984-1989)

From my antenna of the SWOT analysis for AIMA (*vide* Chapter 7 above), the strengthening of relationships with the Asian management body AAMO and the global conglomerate CIOS was an important task.

Since AIMA had been a very active member of AAMO, opportunities came soon. I was to attend AAMO's regional meetings and consultative forums at different points of time, held as follows :

- *Seoul*—Under Korean Management Association (KMA);
- *Tokyo*—Under International Management Association of Japan (IMAJ);
- *Hong Kong*—Under Hong Kong Management Association (HKMA);
- *Manila*—Under the Philippines Council of Management (PHILCOMAN);
- *Kuala Lumpur*—Under Malaysian Institute of Management (MIM);
- *Singapore*—Under Singapore Institute of Management (SIM);
- *Bangkok*—Under Thailand Management Association (TMA);
- *Jakarta*—Under Indonesian Management Association (PERMANIN)
- *Canberra*—Under Australian Institute of Management (AIM) [Incidentally, Bangladesh was not part of AAMO's network

nor did it have a national management association then, but was keen to become active in the management arena. With the initiative from the then Head of the Department of Business Administration, University of Dhaka—(*Bangladesh*) organised an international seminar on "Management in SAARC Countries" and I presented an invited paper on "Status of Management Education in SAARC Countries" covering the scenario.]

All the nine Asia-Pacific metropolises—without a single exception—were "swinging" cities in their own rights and, after the novelty of travel (occasionally more than once to each) to new, exciting places wore off, I realised —- with a slight tinge of regret—that the group never offered to hold a single meeting in the Indian capital !

The reason was not far to find. India had held the Presidency of AAMO in 1968-71, with Dr. K.S. Basu, but nobody thereafter. India had, however, a President of CIOS, Dr. Bharat Ram (1975-78), Chairman, DCM, along with a treasurer, Dr. Ram S. Tarneja, MD, *Times of India* group, for that period. AIMA also hosted CIOS Congress in Delhi in 1978, which was the only AIMA event, in 50 years, which the Prime Minister of India had come to grace. As far as AAMO was concerned, its early beginnings, during the first 15 years of 1960-75, were the times for sharing experience among the few "club" members. The second phase, 1970-80, was characterised by regional activities: designed to secure the regional market. The period saw a clear move to transform AAMO from a "club" into a self-financing organisation. The early 1980s were a period of economic difficulties in the region. Recession, coupled with the emerging difficulties of supporting CIOS—which was undergoing severe constitutional and financial crisis—affected AAMO. Organisational activities virtually ceased and AAMO reverted to "club" status, seeking more members. Each member was left to find for itself alone.

When I joined the fray and chose to lobby for India's Presidency once again for AAMO, this was the position. S.L. Rao (to whom the above analysis is due) was of great help and telephonically suggested the name of Dr. Tarneja for AAMO Presidency. I, in turn, succeeded—particularly with the help of MIM—after a series of meetings in successive countries and Dr. Tarneja was finally nominated as President, 1989-92.

[In 1992, the ninth AAMO Triennial Management Conference

on "The Asia-Pacific Region—Management in Transition" was held in Delhi under the Presidency of Dr. Tarneja and was hailed a grand success. I was then not in AIMA and that I was not even invited, was an entirely different matter.]

× × ×

To set the records straight, since the early 1960s—an era in which Management as a profession and Management Education as a discipline (vide Chapter 1, "Rumblings of IT") were becoming universally recognised and accepted—the World Council of Management (CIOS) had begun as an international organisation, which spread the gospel of management across the globe. AAMO, in fact, had begun in the garb of the Indo-Pacific Council of the Comite International l'Organisation Scientifique (IPC-CIOS). This happened to be one of the regional arms, like CE-CIOS for Europe—now re-named European Management Association (EMA)—and PAC-CIOS for the Americas, for the parental world organisation, CIOS.

In 1986, my contact with CIOS was extremely tenuous and only happened through John Diebold (1926-2005) its President, who was also the President of the American Management Association. A Harvard Business School product and one of the Titans of the American management movement, Diebold was the early promoter of computer systems in business and his visionary thinking on IT helped ushering in computers in the USA. His book, *Automation* (1952), foresaw programmable devices to be in use for everyday operations of many kinds of business. He founded "John Diebold and Associates" (1954), operating on a global plane, which influenced many large American companies into computerising their business. Diebold helped put computers in banking and hospitals. His clients covered cities, states and national governments. "Diebold Institute of Public Policy" (1968) advised on technology issues to help the general public.

In 1986, I had landed in New York for a CIOS official networking and was invited for a "breakfast" meeting with Diebold—cutting through a lot of bureaucratic red tape. The meeting in the breakfast suite of a deluxe hotel went through well and, being told that AIMA's National Management Convention (NMC) was coming up soon in Delhi, Diebold kindly offered to hold a "live" video-teleconference between top managers in the USA and their counterparts in India during our NMC's duration, agreeing to lead the video-teleconference from the West. He also proposed that, for this purpose, the newly launched WORLDNET Satellite could be specially pressed into service: synchronised at the precise hour, minute and second and the connectivity could remain operational for the designated split-second duration for three-quarters-of-an-hour under NASA. All this was breathtakingly new and I was there simply to acquiesce !

While the venue in New York in 1986 was left to be worked out by the US authorities operating the satellite, the video-teleconference venue in Delhi was specially made at the United States Information Services (USIS)—also called the American Center—in a completely instrument-panelled lounge, with a select band of India's top-notch managers (including Chairmen of SAIL and Hindustan Lever, with AIMA President acting as moderator at our end): to "face" their interlocutors of equal eminence in the USA. For the first time ever, a "live" satellite-based video-teleconference took place between two bands of eminent managers from India and the USA—situated thousands of miles apart—in "visible" and "audible" modes over the clockwork-precision of 45 minutes. Other NMC delegates sat in the USIS's adjacent conference hall in rapt attention—to watch the event and listen on a big screen.

[Diebold, all the way from New York, did not forget to mention my name for giving thanks in his own overture, which was so very gracious of him !]

× × ×

In 1987, I called upon Sam Pitroda, in his Spartan office at Akbar Bhavan, to apprise him of our first-ever management video teleconference as above, in the previous year. We immediately took to each other,—I was totally taken in by his charismatic personality and he was happy at the IT penumbra of AIMA due to our humble efforts.

In 1984, when he had first returned to India at the invitation of Indira Gandhi, he had founded the Centre for Development of Telematics (C-DOT), transforming Indian telecommunication and indigenising the massive business of upgrading the archaic telecom system. In 1987, he became Advisor to Rajiv Gandhi, as PM, and headed as many as six technology Missions, namely, Telecommunications, Water, Literacy, Immunisation, Dairy and

Oilseeds. As the first-ever Chairman of Indian Telecommunication Commission, he incubated Public Call Offices (PCOs), making available cheap domestic and international public telephone all over the country.

Born in 1942, settled in Chicago and holding in a few scores of patents in the USA, Pitroda had a wonderful sense of convivial humour. He regaled me by recalling, "I had so much to learn from my adolescent son. I was floored when the little one came and asked me: 'Dad, why are playing cards not digital'? When I asked him to explain, he contemptuously said: 'Look, they are decimal, going 1, 2, 3 and so on. Why can't they be binary as 1, 2, 4 and 8'? I was amazed and set working on what I eventually devised as 'Compucards': a patent earning me zillions of dollars" !

We kept meeting. When, in 1989, Pitroda was leading a high level Government delegation on the theme of "Transition from Controlled Economy to Competitive Economy" to the Second World, he kindly invited me to join the delegation as a member: to present a viewpoint for our kind of freely competitive economy.

The delegation was to visit the erstwhile Soviet countries, with Moscow as the first stop and Riga, Lithuania, as the next stop, The delegation had N. Waghul, Chairman, ICICI, Jerry Pandey, Chief of Citibank and other top men from Indian business and industry as members. Our mentor was the internationally renowned management-guru, Prof C.K. Prahlad, who met us—prior to our deliberations—in Moscow and provided us what he termed a "road map". We had many meetings, presentations and across-the-table dialogues with our Second World counterparts. We returned satisfied after our parleys, having hopefully achieved the given mission: of laying down an untrodden path to our friends.

× × ×

AIMA's credentials in business and industry were already a legion and, now that the "IT wave" had caught on with AIMA, new MDPs could be conceived. One likely collaborator was National Institute of Industrial Engineering (NITIE), situated on the picturesque Powai Lake in Mumbai, a stone's throw from IIT, Mumbai. Dr. S. Ramani, Director of NITIE—with a distinguished management and industrial engineering background—was an equal enthusiast for IT and agreed to collaborate, offering NITIE's spacious campus and ample infrastructural facilities.

Together, we offered the following IT-based courses to Indian management and industry over 1986-89:

- 5-day programme on "Computerised Production Management", with practical projects of IT in production;
- 5-day programme on "Computerised Inventory Management", with practical projects of IT in inventory;
- 5-day programme on "Computerised Project Management", with hands-on modules of IT in project management; and
- 5-day programme on "Computerised Personnel Management", with practical projects of IT in Human Relations.

All the above AIMA-NITIE programmes ran full-house and were regarded as great success.

× × ×

Speaking about IIT Mumbai, the Indian IT story had grown superbly in the direction of academic excellence. Interestingly, the IITs had each a different "godfather": the Soviets for Mumbai; the USA for Kanpur; and Germany for Madras (though none for the first IIT, Kharagpur). It has been commented by Sharma, "IITs became epi-centres of technology excellence, though the fruits did not immediately translate into direct national benefit. The academic mindset that set more store by a doctoral 'dhobi mark' rather than practical applications continued to hamper the IITs for decades".

Prof. V. Sampath, Director of IIT Kanpur, was very aware of the above critical view, howsoever merited or otherwise, and thought it fit to set up a committee for evaluation of its IT and management interface with business and industry. While Dr. Biswajit Nag, Secretary, DoE and Prof. P.V.S. Rao from TIFR were members, I was invited from AIMA to be the third member of the evaluation committee. During several visits, we had a few rounds of discussion with the IT faculty of IIT—led by the redoubtable Prof. V. Rajaraman and Prof. V. Shankar—and ended with a colloquium with the entire IIT faculty—to elicit their valuable views—before formulating our recommendations. We hoped, inter alia, to reduce an apparent corporate bias in coming to the IIT Kanpur, with the following goals:

- To solve nuts-and-bolts problems of the industry at the IT laboratory of IIT in the *short term* and gently persuade the IT faculty not to look down upon industry's mundane areas of front-end usage of technology;
- To invite industry in formulating research collaboration with IT faculty on *long term* basis—for applied research and reverse engineering, among other areas—which could be "Win-Win" situation for both industry (in finding technology solutions to complex problems) and for IT faculty (in preparing academic papers with clear-cut research-findings).

× × ×

Asian Productivity Organisation (APO) was an apex body for industrial productivity and related issues, comprising greater Asia and the Pacific Rim. The social situation in these APO areas were changing in recent years, with the newly industrialised economies (NIEs) taking off in industrialisation. Manufacturing technology in the NIEs—especially in electronics and automobile industries in Korea and elsewhere—achieved international competitiveness. The relative ease of industrialisation and the decrease in value attained through manufacturing industries was an early symptom of an "information society": identifying a stage in societal development.

In view of such social changes and to formulate basic strategies to cope with the emerging structural changes, APO Basic Research on IT was initiated in 1987, since APO was convinced that IT was a powerful tool to promote socio-economic development in member-countries, termed "IT-led development". The research was conducted by a group of six Experts from APO countries. In addition, National Advisers from 11 APO member-courtiers joined in the study and reported on the development status of each country, from the view point of IT-led development. APO's Indian constituent, National Productivity Council (NPC)—nestling in "Productivity House" next door to "Management House" of AIMA—selected me to be the National Adviser from India.

In the 1987 international symposium—held among Experts and National Advisers at Gotemba, located in the picturesque foothill of Mt. Fujiyama in Japan—I presented IT applications in five major areas in India, keeping in view the economic growth of 5.1 per cent in 1986-87 and anticipated increase between 1 per cent and 2 per cent in 1987-88,—carryings out SWOT analysis for each area as follows:

Public Administration Informatics

NIC as premier national organisation with NICNET as wide-area computer network with large regional computers at Delhi, Bhuvaneshwar, Pune, Hyderabad and Chennai: using four NEC and one ND computers; 22 States having computer centres on ECIL mainframe; and 390 district headquarters using PCs and super-minicomputers. NICSAT was the dedicated satellite under NIC.

- *Technology Strength (S)*: Creation of widespread employment opportunities for computer professionals; uniformity in administration of central, State and district information systems, under the NIC network.
- *Technology Weakness (W)*: Deficiency in leadership; lack of subject-knowledge; high cost of dedicated satellite.
- *Societal Opportunity (O)*: Better planning environment under Planning Commission and State planning boards; vastly improved information exchange between Centre and States; spin-off in employment creation in user community for public administration.
- *Societal Threat (T)*: Likely conflict between "top-down" approach of NIC and "bottom-up" approach of the States; likely information monopoly at Centre due to access to State information; likely creation of information dependency on Centre due to India's federal structure.

Natural Resource Informatics

National Natural Resource management System (NNRMS) was planned for natural resources with remote-sensing satellites and a large number of image-processing computers at different locations.

- *Technology Strength (S)*: Immensely rich data-base on various natural resources; ability to retrieve any kind of natural resource; ability to make forecast in space and time.
- *Technology Weakness (W)*: Possibility of poor administration

of data; likely dependence on personal motivation and initiative at micro-level.

- *Societal Opportunity (O)*: Definite improvement in district planning; definite improvement in resource planning; better allocation of resources.
- *Societal Threat (T)*: Likely rivalry among States for scarce resource; High social cost of incorrect usage of resource; likely information monopoly by power groups.

Environmental Informatics

Indian Meteorological Department (IMD) having CRAY-X MP-2 Supercomputer for numerical weather prediction (NWP), based on a complex SACRAMENTO model relating to a vast array of variables like clouds, dust, micro-climate, soil, sub-soil, vegetation and so on.

- *Technology Strength (S)*: Strong aid in complex calculations through array processing; high resolution in spatial distance and time intervals.
- *Technology Weakness (W)*: High cost of acquisition and operation; strong dependence on overseas support.
- *Societal Opportunity (O)*: Better quality of civil administration with confident knowledge; better emergency planning and disaster management for cyclone, flash floods, tidal bores and sea storms; adoption of better agricultural, forestry and animal husbandry practices.
- *Societal Threat (T)*: High social cost of unreliable predictions; likely aberration in information usage by power groups.

Social Justice Informatics

Most State capitals had ECIL computers running crime-criminal information system and automated finger print information system. National Crime Research Bureau ran POLICENET, for rapid, appropriate exchange of data on suspected criminals.

- *Technology Strength (S)*: Availability of massive crime and finger print data; availability of a tested model for social justice information; high uniformity in social justice administration.

- *Technology Weakness (W)*: Likely lack of motivation in systematic data capture; likely distortion in data quality; likely absence of proper leadership; likely usage of data to satisfy individuals.
- *Societal Opportunity (O)*: Vast improvement in crime detection and criminal apprehension; substantial improvement in criminal conviction; efficient information exchange through POLICENET; better social environment and education of crime.
- *Societal Threat (T)*: Likely threat to individual liberty; likely wrong usage by power groups; possible lack of Centre-State and inter-State cooperation.

Economic and Development Informatics

Planning Commission used INTER-DATA computer for detailed material-flow balance in over 80 sectors, using input-output relations, investment, imports, employment and perspective planning. This was done through VIDHATA model for agriculture, exports, demography, investments and deciding long-term objectives. Gujarat used a SUNRAY computer for Integrated Rural Development Projects (IRDPs), Uttar Pradesh used SPERRY-UNIVAC computer for Drought-Prone Area Projects (DPAPs).

- *Technology Strength (S)*: Use of small PCs; use of local language as done in Gujarat; commitment to data quality and information usage by local people.
- *Technology Weakness (W)*: Possible lack of leadership; possible lack of secialised knowledge.
- *Societal Opportunities (O)*: High potential for extension in orchard location, afforestation, seri-culture cultivation, etc.; potential for improved technology transfer ("lab-to-land").
- *Societal Threat (T)*: Likely social cost of incorrect usage; likely information monopoly by power groups.

A single-window concept for all regulatory procedures concerning manufacture of computers, together with liberalised import, marked the Government's IT policy in the late-1980s, as follows:

1. Each application to be cleared within two months;

2. Investment allowance to be given for items covered under new policy;
3. Entire computer industry to be exempt from location policy, in view of its high technology nature;
4. SW development to be regarded as "electronic industry" to get several incentives;
5. Reservation policy for small-scale sector to be given up;
6. Manufacture of micro- and mini-computers to be permitted without nay capacity restriction;
7. Only control was to be through phased manufacturing programme
8. Manufacture of mainframes and super-computers to be restricted to public sector for two years, left to ECIL;
9. Customs duty concessions to be given up;
10. Computer components to be divided into two parts for deciding concessional duties;
11. Indigenously manufactured components to be protected from imports through high protective import duties;
12. Actual users to be permitted import of standard DP systems costing less than Rs. 10 lakhs;
13. Importers to be supplied standard list of 12-18 models permitted for import;
14. Indigenous manufacture of components, CPUs and other sub-systems on OEM basis to be encouraged;
15. Liberal import of designs and drawings to be allowed for systems SW and utility SW.

On the whole, IT had arrived on the developing country scene and had the potential to bring about qualitative changes in the process of development.

× × ×

An incidental benefit to the Experts and National Advisers came in 1987 from a visit to FUJITSU's "Laboratory of the Future" at Gotemba where, we were told, technologies likely to materialise in 20 years' time were looked at, and design and development undertaken. We were taken on the top side of a high glass-dome through which we looked at very spacious floors somewhere down below. One of the first things that struck us up above were the preponderance of a large number of walking and vehicle-bound robots that were moving around on the huge floor below, undertaking and accomplishing various tasks.

Was such massive robotisation the shape of things to come in IT technology in 20 years and beyond ? We wondered.

× × ×

In my SWOT analysis for AIMA, a big threat (T) was the dearth of finances and liquidity. In the planning of revenue, while there was no easy solution, management aptitude tests—which were regular cash-earners—was a likely solution. On receiving the idea in AIMA Council from Prof. Rakesh Khurana, Pro-Vice Chancellor of Indira Gandhi National Open University (IGNOU), I proposed "All India Management Aptitude Testing Service" (AIMATS),—to retain the name of AIMA in it. Although the proposal was approved, it was looked at with a good deal of suspicion in its early days, as too crass and commercial. That it had the potential to become the nation-wide common aptitude test (MAT) for admission to MBA/PGDBM programmes of AICTE-approved and non-approved Business schools of India over a period of time, was not realised well in the beginning.

Prof Khurana left for joining Harvard (USA), his alma mater and I lost a big support in the Council. AIMATS had to wait for another half-a-decade to become a nation-wide MAT and, much more important, a "cash cow" for AIMA, as staff-members put it.

The continued cash-crunch affected in another way. AIMA was expanding fast and the "Management House" needed more space, to say the least. I was trying out in the Lodi Road Institutional Area first for remaining in the vicinity, but was told that the area was exclusively demarcated for the Government offices alone. In Lutyen's Delhi, there was no private land, except far away, such as, in Qutab Institutional Area where Prem Pandhy, an eminent past-President, offered to share with the allotted land for International Management Institute (IMI) that he had started, but AIMA was not keen to go that far.

Meanwhile, the India Habitat Centre (IHC) was to come up next door and I got hold of built-up space there as suggested by friends in the Government. This was in 1988, it was to be a cost of Rs. 1.20 crores and I arranged to deposit the money for initial instalments. There was a lot of opposition, and as soon as I left, AIMA surrendered the prime space in 1992—on the plea that it did not have the money to pay for the remaining instalments. I believe the industry association,

CII, grabbed the space the moment AIMA vacated its hold. It remained a pity because that kind of prime space in near vicinity was never available to AIMA again, while the so-called "cash cow" of AIMATS was staring in the eyes all the while!

× × ×

From the SWOT analysis, a long-range vision for AIMA was needed to be worked out. This kind of exercise had been talked about in the past, but never put down in writing. Meanwhile, we had gained experience from our newly-forged links with the Government: what with Ministries' grants for computerisation and IAS officers' courses and wanted to suggest a "broad-band" expansion of horizon from Industry to government and others.

My worthy colleague Ramaswamy and I sat down in 1988 to build, from scratch, a long-range plan (LRP), somewhat as follows:

> "If the aim of AIMA is the efficient and optimal utilisation of resources, its activities should impinge on all segments of the society's economy, where resources have to be carefully used. Most of AIMA's activities in the past have been focussed on the private sector of industry. It must now begin to reach out to small-scale industry, the public sector, departments and enterprises of the government at the Centre, States and local authorities,, non-governmental organisations, and bodies that have to deliver services, such as, education, health, public distribution, nutrition programmes, family planning, safeguarding the environment and ecology, etc."

Ramaswamy and I followed up the above thoughts with ideas of illustrative functional centres of AIMA:

- *Centre for Management Studies (AIMA-CMS)*: To conduct the distance leaning education and other study programmes;
- *Centre for Management Development (AIMA-CMD)*: To run the management development programmes in diverse sectors;
- *Centre for Management Services (AIMA-CMS)*: To carry out the Aptitude Tests and render IT and other services; and
- *Centre for Management Research (AIMA-CMR)*: To collect

management and administration case-studies and to commission research in sectoral areas.

In 1988, in a truncated executive-board meeting of the Council, held in a posh Mumbai venue in Dr Tarneja's presence, the LRP was discussed and approved within a few minutes. [I have no comments on the extent of Council participation or duration of deliberation for a subject of LRP's importance. I believe, however, that some of our LRP ideas have been worked upon and I wish AIMA well.]

× × ×

[Working with AIMA for nearly five years could not make me immune from observing its funny side. Elected annually, all Council Members—and Presidents—were generally with impeccable professional credentials, apart from being gentle souls and providing the secretariat their gracious guidance. Yet all election processes were prone to vagaries and, even rarely, there could be a vainglorious President, who would have the making of a disaster. One such President, for instance, would collect "important" documents, urging that no copy must be kept back at AIMA secretariat and, a few days later, would revert to say that he had "misplaced" his papers !

During the years that Rajiv Gandhi was the Prime Minister (PM) of India, this President announced in a Council meeting that PM had "agreed" to be the Patron of the forthcoming National Management Convention (NMC) and AIMA's chief executive must make preparations for NMC by painstakingly "obtaining instructions from PM". NMC was an annual event of AIMA and the Council was impressed (which was perhaps the intention) to learn about PM's *prima facie* interest. Days passed, nothing happened, and after much one-way correspondence and solicitous enquiries, Dr. Montek Singh Ahluwalia—the then Special Secretary to PM—confirmed telephonically that PM was not involved in any way. Our President immediately lost all interest in the NMC, though only 45 days were left. It was a Herculean task to pull off the myriad activities of the NMC and, mainly thanks to my energetic colleague, Lalita Iyer, the event could be held finally without any mishap,—to our immense relief. Our President remained unfazed.]

9

IT: Have Wings, Shall Fly ! (1990-2005)

I left AIMA in end-1989 and ceased to be the "caged bird" with clipped wings, as in Tagore's classic poem, *Two Birds*. I became once again the freedom-loving "forest bird" of his verse: spreading liberated wings in the wide, open, professional sky, where free-lancing knew no limits!

× × ×

As is well-known, Rajiv Gandhi (August 1944 - May 1991) was the architect of computers and IT in free India. Even during his years as a pilot with Indian Airlines prior to 1984, he had a lively interest in gadgets—and found a mentor in P.S. Deodhar, who was to set up APLAB, the earliest among Indian test and measurement- equipment makers. Deodhar briefed Rajiv Gandhi on the labyrinthine laws that hamstrung entrepreneurs in India. Rajiv Gandhi carried the message to his mother, Indira Gandhi, the then Prime Minister. Even as he assumed an unofficial role as a computer-friendly facilitator for events like the 1982 Asian Games in Delhi, he smoothed the passage of the major liberalisation that finally came to the IT industry as a gift in August 1983.

During his Prime Ministership in 1984-89, Rajiv Gandhi brought a total change in the Indian communication system. Prior to his era, neither the Indian people nor the Government of India was aware of, or accustomed to, the concept of IT. He perhaps would not be able to take the steps, but for the help of Sam Pitroda whom he brought as his Adviser. An eminent technologist and holder of a large number of patents, Pitroda—originally from Odisha and settled in the USA (vide Chapter 7, "IT-Government Interface")— agreed to come to India, at Rajiv Gandhi's request at a token salary.

Rajiv Gandhi also involved committed technocrats like P.S. Deodhar, N. Sheshagiri and T.H. Chowdhary to take forward his IT vision once he became Prime Minister in 1984, after Indira Gandhi's assassination in the same year. Soon afterwards, as mentioned earlier, Rajiv Gandhi announced a new IT policy, which saw the creation of C-DOT in Delhi under Sam Pitroda to usher in a telecommunication revolution (to provide telephone easily to the common man) and C-DAC in Pune under Vijay Bhatkar to initiate India's first supercomputer, PARAM.

× × ×

One of the best things to happen to me, as I started free-lancing, was chaperoning the World Software Congress in early February 1991 where Rajiv Gandhi was invited to interact with the delegates for a time far exceeding his allotted two-hour span. S.P. Singh Bedi, heading "Indian Software Association", had planned a two-day convention at the Convention Hall of Ashok Hotel and had asked me to be Chief Coordinator. Over the first day and a half, we had lack-lustre deliberations on problems and prospects of Indian SW being produced and reaching the global market, and heard enlightened presentations from personalities like Saurabh Srivastava, MD of IIS Infotech. The only international presence was marked by a small delegation from Central Asia on the second morning, but it did not matter. On the second-day afternoon, Rajiv Gandhi—then the General Secretary of the Indian Congress (after having lost the General Elections, 1989)—joined up and it was wonderful to find him sparing the entire time on a subject, undoubtedly close to his heart.

I moderated the entire event as Compere standing on the podium and a spirited interaction ensued—with a smiling Rajiv Gandhi seated on the rostrum and a very involved audience lapping up every word of his—that lasted the whole afternoon. The dialogue went somewhat on the following lines:

Q. Before you became PM in 1984, when you first wanted to introduce computers in India, what was the criticism you faced?

A. You see, Left political parties throughout the country launched demonstrations. They propagated that computer was a "super-robot" and a single computer would finish the job of at least 100 labours ! As a result, there would be acute job loss for the people. Out of this fear, the Left State Government of West Bengal resisted entry of computer in that State and forbade computer from coming in for at least 10 years !

Q. As PM in 1984-89, you brought with you brightness and hope, as well as a believable vision of the twenty first century. What did you want to project?

A. I tried to project an image of modernity. I tried to infuse a new confidence among people, which would be relying heavily on science and technology. I have been dubbed as a man in hurry! But I aspired to make my country a technologically advanced nation. This was to happen in the next two decades, with the inputs of modern science and technology.

Q. Your name has been synonymous with the ushering in of Computer Revolution in India !

A. Thank you.

Q. You gave us a call to take us into the twenty first century. What was your dream ?

A. My dream was of modernising India. I wanted to bring our country technologically, economically, socially—into the new millennium. Mine was dream of a strong and proud and united India. I wanted India to march into the twenty first century with courage and confidence. If permitted, I wanted to be a crusader of modern science and technology.

Q. Your inspiring vision has been in clear and confident terms, but you have often contradicted the discourse of your time. Is that right ?

A. I have been always frank. My zeal has been for effective utilisation of science and technology towards our welfare. I have always realised that modern science and technology can play a useful role in social uplift. It can create a more open society. It can bring India closer together.

Q. One last question, which is the computer system you have?

A. It is a Sinclair (?) computer, with so much RAM, so much ROM, and so many peripherals... (His way of giving rapid-fire details evoked all-round mirth and brought the dialogue to a fitting close.)

[Throughout the scintillating Q&A session, Rajiv Gandhi maintained a very relaxed appearance. He would occasionally wink at me from across the rostrum: either to allow the questioner to go on, or, subtly indicate to make him stop! It was a most memorable experience and nothing—literally nothing—made us guess at that moment that we would have to lose this most forward-looking and yet most genial icon of Indian youth within as short a time as subsequent one hundred days, under the most tragic of circumstances.]

One of the most heartening legacies that Rajiv Gandhi left was the trail taken up by the unlikely State of Assam and that is worth putting on records, on the following lines:

Initiative

Rajiv Gandhi Computer Literacy Programme (RGCLP) was a unique educational venture with private sector participation. Assam's Planning and Development and AMTRON, the State nodal agency for IT, embarked on the ambitious project of providing computer education—free of cost—to the students of government schools. AMTRON tied up with NIIT and CMC, and covered, in the first three phases, all the 630 higher secondary schools across Assam. The challenge was not only to provide IT literacy to all the school children, but also to help building a new generation of talent that would have a changed mind-set.

Process

The Build-Operate-Transfer (BOT) model—used in road construction and elsewhere—was created around infrastructure creation, system integration, facilities management, education delivery, student learning and teachers training. Each school was equipped with the IT paraphernalia: computer HW, licensed SW, external modem, dot-matrix printer, UPS, switch, suitable SW for sharing the Internet, computer desks and chairs, printer platforms, instructor tables and chairs, power and generating set. The IT education was facilitated by two faculty members. The "Microsoft Shiksha Programme" helped regular subject teachers to gain required computer skills, which helped them to impart computer-aided education. The required course content, including computer-based learning (CBT) for computer-aided learning (CAL) and spoken English, was provided to each school.

The faculty used NetMeeting as a regular teaching tool, while addressing a large group of children.

Impact

RGCLP helped in spreading computer literacy across all sections of the society, especially to the poor and rural students: hitherto denied an opportunity to learn on computers. It provided an opportunity for the community to earn on computers after school hours, which helped immensely in bridging the "digital divide". It helped students in gaining necessary command over the language with the help of the spoken English module: a part of the RGCLP deliverables. Computers were also used to teach non-computer science subjects. Finally, new employment opportunities were provided to more than 1,300 youths, besides training 15,240 teachers under the "Shiksha" programme.

Many other States followed the RGCLP-like paradigms, and it would be worthwhile to assess how far India gained in imparting IT education to school students, as fitting homage to Rajiv Gandhi—the truest architect of IT in modern India—whom I was so singularly lucky to interact with, from such close quarters at the Ashok Convention Hall, one February afternoon.

× × ×

On a global praxis, the human society has evolved continuously from its pre-industrial, to industrial and finally to post-industrial manifestation. An alternative way of looking at the evolving society is to divide it among the following sectors:

1. Primary (Agriculture) Society — with a focus on nature;
2. Secondary (Industry) Society — with a focus on material;
3. Tertiary (Service) Society — with a focus on community;
4. Quaternary (Leisure) Society — with a focus on individual.

Over time, there has been a perceptible shift from the agriculture society to the service society, and now to leisure society (also called information society). This has been evident both in the developed world as well as the newly industrialising world of India.

In September 1991, CSI held a Working Conference as a precursor to its National Convention on "IT in Everyday Life". The objective was to have: (1) presentations by subject-area specialists from user organisations from all the four sectors; and (2) consolidation of recommendations for action.

I was invited to be the Convenor of the 2-day Working Conference and we made out the following participant-profile:

1. Primary Society (Focus on Nature)

Crops and Seeds	: Indian Council of Agricultural Research
Agriculture	: DoE
Water resources	: Central Water Commission
Rural Development (General)	: Ministry of Agriculture
Rural Development (CRISP)	: NIC
Decentralise Planning (DISNIC)	: NIC
Weather & Environment	: India Meteorological Department
Environment	: Ministry of Environment & Forestry
Desk-top Mapping	: Systems Research Institute.

2. Secondary Society (Focus on Material)

Manufacturing	: Knowledge Engg. & Consultancy Services
Steel	: Steel Authority of India (SAIL)
Oil	: Oil India Ltd. (OIL)
Oil & Natural Gas	: ONGC
Coal	: Coal India Ltd.
Power	: Central Electricity Authority (CEA).

3. Service Society (Focus on Communities)

• Banking	: State Bank of India (SBI)
• General Insurance	: General Insurance Corporation (GIC)
• Health	: Centre for Bio-medical Engg,, IIT Delhi and All-India Institute of Med. Sc. (AIIMS)

Education (CLASS Project)	: NCERT
Telecommunications	: MTNL
Intelligent Building	: CMC Ltd.
Road	: Delhi Transport Corporation (DTC)
Railways	: Ministry of Railways
Airlines	: Indian Airlines
Police (General)	: National Crime Records Bureau (NCRB)
Police (Finger Print identification)	: NCRB
Employment	: Dte. Gen. of Employment & Trg. (DGE&T)

4. Leisure Society (Focus on Individual)

Newspapers & Magazines	: Cyber Media Ltd.
Television	: Dte. Gen. of Doordarshan
Books	: NIIT Ltd.
Indian languages	: Odisha Comp. Appln. Centre (OCAC)
Art & Culture	: NIC and IGNCA
Games & Sports	: NIC and Sports Authority of India (SAI)

The 35 participant organisations interacted closely with one another in panel discussions and user-review sessions, leading to the following recommendations:

A. Achievements and Experience

1. Achievements for IT use in key economic sectors to be recorded;
2. Need of documentation and publication on benefits of IT;
3. Loss saved and service improved to be highlighted;
4. SAIL experience to be recorded on efficient resource utilisation; and
5. SAIL experience to make IT vendor work needing highlighting.

B. IT Use Strategy

1. Need of a national time-table for POLICENET;
2. Scope for adopting pre-planning in employment orientation;
3. Ministry of Surface Transport to develop comprehensive IT plan;
4. NIC's experience on construction projects to be noted by CEA;
5. "Trojan Horse" approach instead of grand plan for IT usage;
6. Accountability needed for commitments in CLASS programmes; and
7. IT user forum needed for all vendor-related IT issues.

C. Integration of IT Material

1. Integrated village-level data needed instead of separate surveys;
2. DISNIC to integrate 29 State-level district information collections;
3. CSI to give tariff-reduction suggestions to Chelliya Committee;
4. Integrated action plan needed for CWC into a national schedule;
5. Ministry IT plans needed to be part of national IT action plan; and
6. CSI to help formulating plan for improving quality of life.

D. Training and Standardisation

1. CSI to make check-list on preparations for computer purchase;
2. DoE to lay down good documentation standards for HW, SW;
3. CSI to determine "Code of Ethics" for all IT vendors;
4. Need of a training institute for banking information; and
5. NIC's CAI centres using Multi-Media needed on priority basis.

E. Action Plan

1. Time-bound action-plan needed for using "public domain" SW;

2. Single "clearing house" needed to avoid overlap of projects;
3. NIC to help all non-profit, NGO and research agencies; and
4. UNDP-supported CAM and CAD SW projects to make documentation public.

On the whole, the lesson that emerged was that both CSI and DoE should orchestrate and catalyse together a lot of disjointed IT efforts in the country. But were there any takers ?

× × ×

Ever since the 1960s, when third-generation computers started having operating systems (OS), Systems SW was "bundled" with HW by the IT professionals, to enhance the utilitarian value of the computer. For the end-users, however, most of the application programs were "customised" (i.e., made to suit specific needs). There were other application packages, which had general applicability across multiple machines. As "general application packages" began to be tested with several user-managers and their views obtained on the shortfalls and needed modifications, these comments were closely worked upon for further development. With recursive testing and feedbacks, the packages could be improved as to have almost universal applicability—in order to become globally available "products".

Due, however, to the expensive nature of launching and sustaining the above testing and feedback process in a recursive manner, India had not been conspicuously successful to launch many "products". Although help was organised by the government and the private sector to organise extensive testing, de-bugging and "hand-holding", examples of really successful "products" have been rare. In one such endeavour by the public-sector ET&T Corporation, initiated by their forward-looking CMD, BC Mahanty, I was the concerned Consultant in 1990 onwards.

In the selection and evaluation process, we sought the basic information as follows :

(i) *Technical Information*—Minimum HW requirement for OS; menu-driven (preferred by managers) or command-driven (preferred by SW professionals); nature of "help" provided to the user; operating options (additions, deletions, messages); scope of backtrack; frequency of "bugs"; "help" through windows; likely support from developer/vendor for future updating; copy protecting; special points.

(ii) *Market Information*—Availability of similar software; competitor's SW with quality and price; corporate image of the developer/vendor; list of other customers (if available).

(iii) *Training Information*—Availability of manuals; availability of tutors; availability of demonstration package; expected training time.

(iv) *General Comments*—Plus and minus points to be summarised.

A market-survey in India in the early 1990s yielded the following packages and products and their approximate price-range:

- *Medical and Hospital Package*—There were three categories: large hospitals of 200-300 beds or more; nursing homes and polyclinics with 50-1oo beds or so; and doctors' chambers with occasional provision of private beds. In the first category, all the necessary modules existed, e.g., out-patient management, in-patient admission management; ward management, paramedical staff management, medicine and stores management, doctor's appointment system, facilities management, operations theatre management and financial management. Some advanced packages even maintained disease-wise records: from diagnosis to cure (or fatality). The second category was a watered-down version of the above. Doctor's chambers package mainly emphasised patient history and medication.

  Price-range varied widely. For Centre for Railway Information System (CRIS), price was Rs.1.0 lakh. For Jaypee's HOMPAC, very user-friendly and very modular, it was expensive, around Rs, 3.0 lakhs. HMS packages from ASCI, Hyderabad and RCC, Chandigarh, were good, but not comprehensive. For individual doctors, DOCPAC by R&D Market Men, Chennai, although not comprehensive, was priced at Rs. 10,000.
- *Financial Package*—They were broadly two varieties. The large ones were for business houses, covering all financial accounts like journals, ledgers, trial balance, profit and loss account, and balance sheet. The smaller category was meant for individual shops and department stores.

TCS in the first category offered an excellent package EX around Rs. 8,000. Pentonics, Chennai, offered TALLY, very good and interfaced with inventory, at Rs. 12,000. Another one, very user-friendly from Quiller Corporation was TOUCH-KEY at Rs.11,000 and FACT from Vedika Corporation in the same range. HISAB for a smaller category from Goenkas, Chennai, was for Rs. 500 and MUNIMJI from Saxenas, Mumbai, was for Rs. 900.

- *Educational Package*—Of three available categories, the first concerned administration of universities, colleges and schools with modules like fee- accounting, library, admission, registration, payroll and time-tabling. The second category was related to examination result-processing and listing of results and mark-sheets. The third was computer-assisted learning (CAL) and computer-based training (CBT).

  In first category, MISS package from Computers, Bangaluru, offered high promise at Rs. 8,000—accepted by University Grants Commission (UGC). In second category, while individual secondary and higher secondary boards (like UPSEB, Bihar SEB, WBSEB) had customised needs, the examination-conducting package of VINYAS from NCST, Mumbai—for examination-conducting passage from a randomised question-bank—was marketed very well. Among CBT packages, CUBE from Computers, Bangaluru, was found very text-book dependent. Among smaller CBT packages, U-LEARN (for learning UNIX) and C-LEARN (for learning C Language) were priced at Rs. 600 each, but again very textbook-bound. CAD-TEACHER from Vision Lab, Hyderabad, was found suitable for teaching in engineering colleges.

- *Law Package*—For allocation of daily business and administration of Registrar's office, Supreme Court, High Courts and District courts, NIC had done exemplary work. In second category, JUDIPACK package was marketed by R&D Market Men, Bangaluru, at Rs. 10,000, but found to be mostly scratch-pad kind and not comprehensive. LAWMAN package form Plus Computers was small and sold at Rs. 8,000. JUDIS package from DT&T sold data-bases for Rs. 5,000 each to lawyers.
- *Engineering Package*—Such packages for design, stress-strain analysis, structural drawings, pipe-laying and instrumentation

diagrams and drafting packages were of consistently high demand among engineering industries, process industries, architectural firm, civil construction companies and mechanical engineering firms, beads engineering colleges and training institutions.

Vision Lab, Hyderabad, launched VISION DESIGNER package at Rs. 20,000 suitable FOR 2-D and 3-D, in competition with AUTO-CAD from Autodesk Corporation, USA. At a lower end, MAC-CAD was introduced by Mac System, Chennai at Rs. 8,000, which was comprehensive for 2-D alone and user-friendly.

- *Office Automation Package*—Large and medium business offices needed office automation for high productivity, follow-up on assigned tasks and day-to-day diaries and directories.

  Cistems, Delhi, offered CISMAIL at Rs. 700 with limited facilities. I-OFFICE from Integra System, Bangaluru, was quite comprehensive and on UNIX platform at Rs. 12,500. In the medium range, EXECUTIVE DESK package from Sofiplus, Mumbai, had all desired features, user-friendly and available at Rs. 1,000.

- *Desk-top Publishing Package*—DTP packages for book design, page-layout and graphic insertions were needed by large and medium book-publishers, newspaper offices and magazine-publishers, besides large business and industry houses needing bulky publications.

  VISION PUBLISHER from Vision Lab, Hyderabad, was offered as a command-driven (and not menu-driven) package. Hindi DTP package, LIPIKA, was embedded into the PAGE MAKER package from the USA, doing well.

- *Travel and Tourism Package*—This package was the need of travel agents, other than large business houses to do travel plans on duty and on leisure.

  CRIS, Delhi, attempted at Rs. 120 the SMART package, which was tested and found to be interactive, but it foundered on the problem of Railways and the airlines frequently changing their travel-schedules. At that low price, such changes could hardly be updated and sent out to customers. But the package had immense potential and remained to be exploited.

× × ×

My relationships with the private as well as public sectors both grew with time. IIS Infotech Ltd—in their many incarnations since 1990—had invited me to remain their Chairman, Governing Council of Academic Affairs. At the beginning, it was called ISCT, an IT education services company with many franchisees in the north and south India. It proliferated into SW export with amalgamation of IIS. Between 1997 and 2000, the UK-based FI International—which had morphed into FI Group in 1988—acquired IIS Infotech Ltd, the Indian computer services company, together with OSI, a London based business consultancy and management support services company and Druids, a Reading-based IT consultancy firm. In April 2001, the total company had the name changed to an esoteric morph: XANSA.

XANSA (India)—in common with XANSA (UK), XANSA (Europe) and other international XANSAs—had four main areas of activities marked out for it:

- Business and technology consultancy;
- IT services;
- Business process outsourcing; and
- IT outsourcing.

But the major preoccupations of XANSA (India) continued to be software development, applications management, export project services and product support, with a pioneering interest in education. Our Governing Council for Academic Affairs comprised —- other than XANSA (India)'s own leadership provided by Rohit Chand, Saurabh Srivastava and Mohit Goyal—a few outside IT stalwarts, such as, Prof. A.R. Kidwai, Vice-Chancellor of Jamia Milia University, Pradeep Gupta, MD, Cyber Media (of DATAQUEST fame); Prof. R.K. Arora of IIT Delhi; and Brig S.V.S. Chowdhry (Retd.), ex-President, CSI and IETE. So the academic climate was strong and we debated, among other things, on the overall education strategy, the role of new SW product modules in education and application potential of new education tools of CAI and CAL coming up.

One of my enduring academic domains was to evaluate the "courseware" that was ever changing and needed fresh updating in every quarter or so. These could be C++ Applets (downloaded from the Net); the growing claim of supremacy tussled between "C" products and "Net" products: UNIX applications of both Berkley Enhancements and Santa Cruz Operations (SCO) versions; and Sun

Microsystems' efforts to develop OS out of a large number of its JAVA language run-time library of programing routines. One common point of academic development was a large-scale endeavour going on, all the time, to bring computers closer to the user and remove—as far as possible—the mystical OS that began in 1964 to support application SW.

My three primary points of concern for user-friendly "courseware" were always as follows:

1. Provision of plenty of graphics;
2. Worked-out examples of various steps; and
3. "How-to" kind of instructions.

[I ceased to be with XANSA (India) from early 2003 when IT education was given up by XANSA as a global line of business.]

× × ×

In January 2003, I was elected as Sectional President of Indian Science Congress for its "Information and Communication Science and Technology" Section. In my Sectional President's address on "Information and Communication in India: Policy to Practice", I noted that in tandem with the rest of the globe, Indian professionals had come to the forefront of IT, leading to not merely to a majority stake in NASA and Microsoft in the USA, but also gaining an influential voice in the Silicon valley there. But within India, I pointed to the disturbing questions as to whether IT policy was sufficiently conducive to make India a world power. Did Indian policy framework facilitate IT being an effective instrument for enhancing economic growth, improving the quality of governance and affecting the core of all planning: reduction of poverty?

I referred to a recent McKinsey Report that there were vital constraints on economic growth in India and that the growth-rate of the national GDP could be hiked by 4 per cent if one could remove the following barriers to growth:

- **Product-market barriers**—These existed in sectors like power, telephone, banking, hotel, retailing, manufacturing, mining, sugar and textile. These barriers accounted for about 2.3 per cent of the obstacles to growth;

- **Land-market barrier**—They related to construction, hotel resorts and retail-trade industries, accounting for 1.3 per cent of the barrier factor;
- **Government ownership**—The balance barriers were in areas like airlines, banking, insurance, manufacturing, mining, power and telecommunication.

By systematic removal of these barriers, it was possible to raise growth-rate from 6 per cent to 10 per cent in Indian economy.

I reported a significant policy announcement by the Secretary to the Ministry of IT that outlined the following policy initiatives—addressing some of the above issues—in September 2001:

1. **IT-for-masses policy**—The Indian population had a top layer of 30 per cent—comprising the affluent as well as the educated—who could handle the most advanced computing systems. There was a second layer of 30 per cent that was educated but not affluent, and one had to cross the poverty barrier there. Yet another 40 per cent were poor living in scattered locations, did not know the '3Rs' and had no access to regular power supply. For them the barriers were three-fold: poverty, illiteracy and energy. The Media Lab Asia—drawn in conjunction with the MIT, USA and gaining from their Media Lab experiment—was an ambitions 10-year, Rs. 5,000 crores plan for meeting the ground challenges in learning, health and enterprise. The funds were to come from Government of India; foundations and private sources; and World Bank and public institutions,—with a one-year exploratory budget. The distributed paradigm, driven from the bottom up by projects and operations at the village level, was expected to provide a vibrant organisational model. [The collaborative aspect of Media Lab Asia project was discontinued later, amalgamating it with the government's on-going plan of activities.]
2. **User-friendly computing devices**—In order that the illiterate could make use of computers, one should have menu-driver, icon-driver, touch-activated and voice-supportive devices, so that the productivity was raised in whatever jobs one did. Some steps in that direction were taken by the BANARAS project conducted by Ranjit Makkuni of XEROX Media Lab

in India,—using bicycle handle to have "walk-through" among Varanasi landmarks, navigating among the architectural surroundings and the scriptural chants, "touching" the arts and artifacts abounding in Varanasi; and myriad other objects and processes. Many of these devices were available much beyond their cultural and spiritual domains, and could be easily adopted for day-to-day information activities.

3. **E-Infrastructure**—There was a vision for providing information-infrastructure, capable of delivering band-widths to every school, college and university in India in accordance with their needs. There were, in all, 237 universities, 1200 engineering colleges, 250 medical colleges and 9 lakhs higher secondary schools in this country, and the Tenth Five-Year Plan sought to network them. [This was a mammoth task and, considering multi-tiered networking of computers, including special provision for the North-East India;—this has remained a pipe-dream].
4. **E-Security**—Foolproof security was necessary for transactions occurring in e-payment systems and "smart cards". The relevant laws were now in position in the IT Act of 2000, where the digital signature regime, along with Public Key Infrastructure (PKI) was envisaged. Under the new office of Controller of Certifying Authorities in the MIT, the process of establishing regional: certifying authorities was now on. Transactions were expected to begin involving digital signature.
5. **Cyber-Security**—This was transactional security related to e-commerce carried out on the Internet. What was involved was network security and production of critical information infrastructure through various "firewalls". [The Internet has continued to be quite porous and a lot of work needs be done here].
6. **Telemetry Policy**—There were two applications involved. First was electronic metering at all load dispatch centres,—leading eventually to remote reading of electronic meters, automatic billing and smooth recovery of the billed dues by the power utilities. The second was terrestrial broadcasting, which had the potential of considerably reducing surplus manpower in public broadcasting, as had been achieved in the UK.

7. **GIS Policy**—Geographical Information System (*vide* "IT Overview" below) was of considerable relevance to watershed management, watershed development, soil conservation programmes, frontline management, disaster management and traffic control. In this wide spectrum could also be included the urban public utility planning where a broad array of agencies worked in over-ground and under-ground modes, and often clashed in their digging and development work. NIC had started to use GIS in metropolitan Delhi in select localities and the work called for wide emulation in other urban regions. The other area was the online real-time pollution control intervention system: using on-line monitoring of ambient air quality (for C, S and N) and the size of solid particulate matter, and real-time intervention to cut off power supply of the polluting units.
8. **e-Commerce**—According to the report of Boston Consulting Group (CG), the global e-commerce transaction were likely to reach $6.8 trillion by 2005. In India, the e-commerce transaction levels would touch Rs. 195,000 crores ($ 40 billion), which is equivalent to our total export today! While the Internet could handle this volume of e-commerce, specific recording of one's priorities and empowerment was called for,—maximising profits, minimising costs and improving cost advantages, as follows:
   - ***Supply Chain Management* (SCM):** To bring into account procurement and distribution efficiency that results in comparative cost advantage. This came from a conscientious networking among ancillary suppliers, production people, inventory managers and finance persons to use a tight coupling of just-in-time supply and virtually zero-inventory.
   - ***Customer Relation Management* (CRM):** To bring about a deeper relationship between the client company and the customer, using the Internet. For instance, if Telco as a client company decided to go for CRM, it should follow a customer through his entire usage-cycle of the vehicle he had bought, right to the level it needed servicing and spare parts, and also meeting the requirement of sale of the vehicle and repurchase of a new one. The brand

loyalty one could build thus to retain a customer was much less than the cost of acquiring a new customer. CRM even enabled—as the LEVI Jeans proved—to do customised designing and giving customers sense of involvement (*vide* "IT Overview" below)!

- ***Enterprise Resource Planning:*** To bring about a high volume of Business-to-Business (B2B) transactions, apart from the fairly large volume of Government-to-Government (G2G), Government-to-Business (G2B) and Government-to-Citizen (G2C) transaction. All these were part of logical outcome of e-commerce once the enabling mechanisms were in position.

× × ×

Over 15 years cr so, between 1990 and 2005, I was intermittently invited as Advisor and Consultant in public or private sectors, to pool IT experience in industry and academics. Only high points are recapitulated below:

Public Sector

- *National Open School (NOS), Delhi*—In keeping with its operative spirit to throw open doors to all school dropouts and the disadvantaged class, the innovative Chairman of NOS, Prof. Marmar Mukhopadhyay, visualised bringing out CDs on "Computers for All", with ample illustrations and easy-to-operate steps. In the days where computers had become ubiquitous, low-priced CD (one or two) would have been the right release for a wide open market. [We could, however, not complete the work due to Mukhopadhyay leaving the position on transfer.]
- *Odisha Computer Application Centre (OCAC), Bhubaneshwar*—Thanks to the initiatives of the IT-savvy Director, Subash Pani, OCAC could undertake many state-of-the-art computer applications, the principal one being land-records keeping with Patwaris in the local *sarala* language which all farmers could understand and hold against misuse by vested interests. [It was an emotional pleasure to witness the Director consecrate the first copy of OCAC

documentation at the feet of Lord Jagannath's idol during the grand *Rathayatra* Festival.]

- *Electronics and Software Promotion Council (ESPC), Delhi*—Concerned at the country-wide deficiency of IT manpower, at all levels of qualification, pointed out by major studies, ESPC commissioned me for a major IT manpower planning study. In carrying out the study, I aimed at the deficiency of the proportionate faculty that would be required for teaching IT manpower and visualised creation of four regional "Indian Institutes for Information technology" (IIIT) that would operate as technical teachers training institutes (TTTIs) exclusively for IT personnel to meet such faculty-deficiency, over and above the Chandigarh and Bhopal TTTIs. [Ironically, large IT centres at university level, also termed IITs, have since come up, but as yet there has been no all-India attempt to meet exclusively the IT faculty-deficiency, as anticipated in our ESPC study.]
- *Centre for Railway Information System (CRIS), Delhi*—I had a close association with CRIS, ever since the time CMC had developed for the Railways its on-line passenger reservation system, IMPRESS. Indian Railways had the largest Rail network in Asia and IMPRESS provided an admirable service—train-wise, station-wise, date-wise, class-wise and quota-wise—striking at the roots of inefficiency and corruption, apart from providing the much-needed relief from clerical drudgery, in the teeth of a phenomenal expansion in the number of trains and passengers. We observed that the other computer communications network for managing Freight Operations Information System (FOIS) did not seem to be such a success, although under gestation for a long time for Central and Zonal systems. FOIS covered movement of wagons, locomotives and containers across the country and haltage at the yards, goods-sheds and loco maintenance sheds.
- *National Crime Records Bureau (NCRB), Delhi*—I had a long-standing relationship with NCRB in their laudable efforts at crime-criminal information system (based on personal details, nature of crime, past records of apprehension/conviction and distribution of crime) and fingerprint information system (based on the digits, whorls and rings, as recorded). NCRB

coordinated both the systems,—beginning with teleprinter-based query and response and, later on, dovetailed into POLICENET computer network across the entire country.

Private Sector

- *Institute for Management Technology (IMT), Ghaziabad*—Under the business house of Kamal Nath, this was already a thriving centre of excellence. At Nath's suggestion, I was invited to look at their teaching modules of IT and suggest improvement, if any. They had an IT-savvy senior person, Col. Suri, with whom it was a pleasure to share knowledge of IT packages and products that could make a difference in IMT's quality of teaching.
- *Swadeshi Polytex Ltd., Ghaziabad*—Belonging to the Swadeshi group of textile enterprises of the Jaipurias, this mill seemed to be still using DCM Data Products' GALAXY-32 systems, under the advice of some consultants and needed urgent modernisation with the cheap and efficient technology available in the market. I proposed a phased plan of IT modernisation, and put them in touch with some computer vendors: available to help.
- *Rollatainers Ltd., Faridabad*—This was a forward-looking company that introduced complete packaging systems to its customers, as the largest producer of lined cartons; it had manufactured and installed 500 packaging machines in India and abroad. Besides its standard in-house applications of accounting, payroll and inventory, we introduced automated capacity planning and scheduling: to put capacity to optimally efficient use. But the main task was to change over to ORACLE at the back-end (from the USA based GUPTA SQL server) and DEVELOPER 2000 at the front-end, since ORACLE-DEVELOPER was known to be a technically strong coupling. Also, we evaluated the global Enterprise Resource Planning (ERP) packages available in the market and arrived at the Hyderabad based RAMCO ERP as the best for Rollatainers.
- *Bhadrachalam Paperboards Ltd., Secunderabad*—This was an Indian supplier of paper, pulp, board, pulp paper, engineering equipment and process chemicals. An integrated

enterprise, it ran as a process industry: from acquisition of timbers onwards to the making of the boards and supply to the market. Under the banner of the ITC group, it followed many enlightened practices. It was easy to apply the process industry norms—in terms of input-output, rejection, wastage, profitability analysis, etc.—and suggest an IT plan to their well-informed MD, KL Chugh.

× × ×

At another level, there were continued spells of IT knowledge sharing in these 15 years with many academic institutions of repute. A brief recapitulation is given below:

- ***Management Development Institute (MDI), Gurgaon***—In this well-reputed academic body, National Management Programme (NMP) was run on a unique shared basis between the private corporate and the public sector. Under SL Rao's Executive Directorship, I was invited to do a self-contained IT course, followed by examination and evaluation.
- ***Indian Institute of Planning and Management (IIPM), Delhi/ Gurgaon***—At the request of their Director, Dr Malay Chaudhuri, I ran a comprehensive Management Information System (MIS) programme, with examination and evaluation, liberally incorporating Indian experiences, for some years from the mid-1990s onwards till the early 2000s.
- ***FORE School of Management (FORE), Delhi***—As suggested by their Evening Director, I ran an MIS course, in the end of 1990s, with mature MBA students in the evening for two years and helped them to conduct actual case studies in live situations. The case studies were documented.
- ***International Management Institute (IMI), Delhi***—Under their Director Dr. Nitish Sengupta, I conducted an evening 30-hour programme for mature MBA students (Final Year, seconded from Industry) on "Management Strategy for IT" in 1999 and 2000.
- ***Jawaharlal Nehru University (JNU), Delhi***—I ran a 30-hour course for MCA (Final Year) students on "Management Strategy for IT" in 2001.[Both the IMI and JNU experiences came handy in honing a similar course for the Post Graduate

(Final Year) students of China's major universities in 2002-03, *vide* Chapter 12.]

- *Guru Govind Singh Indraprastha (GGSIP) University, Delhi*—In 2004 and 2005, I joined their School of Information Technology as Student Advisor, at the suggestion of Prof. K.K. Agarwal, Vice-Chancellor. My task was to provide placement and career advice to the bright, passed out students in terms of likely fitment in industry and corporate houses, depending on their aptitude and interest. It was a new kind of sharing of experience that culminated in conducting a colourful Industry-academic colloquium on "Software Engineering" over two days.
- ***KLG Systel, Gurgaon***—In 2006, there was an unusual extension of my earlier GGSIP University linkage from their MD, Kumud Goel, who sought my advice to evaluate, on-line, "iCarnegie", the Internet-based, copy-protected IT courseware of the Carnegie-Melon University, USA, at a specified price. KLG Systel's notion was that the evaluated and updated courseware (modified, if necessary, by adding elucidatory modules) could be introduced at the GGSIP University, School of IT, curriculum and elsewhere. Although, on the whole, "iCarnegie", the Carnegie-Melon courseware, was excellent, such off-beat purchase of courseware was not workable in the Indian university system, as we sadly found out.

Similar exercises of IT knowledge sharing had gone on for much longer spells—spread over the 1990's—for the public sector giant, National Thermal Power Corporation (NTPC), primarily at their Power Management Institute (PMI), NOIDA. A typical idea of their commitment to computer planning and management could be gauged from my involvement at PMI for the following:

- Planning Computer Configuration;
- Evaluation and Selection of Hardware, Software and Services;
- Financial Management of Computer Centre and Services; and
- Computer System Standards and System Audit.

Based on their burgeoning interest in IT, I was also asked to make several lecture-trips to their picturesque power-project sites at Rihand,

Singhrauli, Shaktinagar and Badarpur: to bring IT knowledge to the doorsteps of managers. Degree of participation could be far more at the project sites.

[Bharat Heavy Electricals Ltd (BHEL) tried out an interesting variation at the level of general managers and below: "Parallels between Developing Managers and *Guru-Shishya Parampara*", in knowledge-sharing with the following criteria:

1. Organisational Climate for Development,
2. Management System and Style, and
3. Key Concepts of Development.

Urging me to share platform with the noted Odissi danseuse Madhavi Mudgal and to illustrate how a common ethos could be shared in IT, management and performing arts!]

Just as Delhi University (Faculty of Management Studies, FMS), Roorkee University, Aligarh University and Maharshi Dayanand University had their needs of practice-based inputs on HW, SW and Network applications, so had NIC, CMC on one side; and IITs (Kanpur, Kharagpur, Mumbai) and IIMs (Ahmedabad, Lucknow, Bangaluru) on the other side. It was exhilarating to share knowledge with all of them that could stand the test of time !

× × ×

A major task of compiling the history of IT education in India—in all its ramifications—was needed to be accomplished at some stage and it was quite appropriate that All India Council of Technical Education (AICTE) came forward to fulfil this task. In 1995, Institution of Electronics and Telecommunication Engineers (IETE) was commissioned by AICTE to carry out the work. At the behest of IETE President, Brig. S.V.S. Chowdhry (Retd.), I was invited to be the Editor.

The resultant 1996 study, "Computer Education in India—Past, Present and Future", was the first of its kind and dealt with the subject of IT education in the whole country: from its earliest stage and well up to the domain of distant future. Divided into five logical parts, the study was done as follows :

- ***Early Development***—We enumerated the emergence of computer HW and SW right from its inception,—as seen through the eyes of very senior IT professionals. It made fascinating reading, since many of them actually participated in the process. Computer education was a concomitant factor which spread its wings to support, as well as sustain, the newly born IT.

- ***Formal Education Scenario***—Here we mapped out the growth and progress of computer education in India: as an accumulated effort of many academic institutions. The scenario was built up from the lowest level of schools to the highest level of Post-Graduate discipline and advanced research. We also covered the education scene in the polytechnics, engineering colleges, IITs (serving as centres of excellence), some central universities (like IGNOU and JNU) and a few deemed universities.
- ***Continuing Education Scenario***—In recognition of the fact that formal education could never cover the total IT education needs of India, we brought out the valuable contributions made by many organisations, institutions, non-academic bodies, professional societies, government departments, public sector enterprises and the whole gamut the private sector. CSI and IETE had played as important roles as NIC and CMC, as also defence sector and many public sector bodies.
- ***Significant Documents***—India owed its debt of gratitude to many visionaries, opinion-leaders and political as well as scientific luminaries who had—from time to time—laid down the need, nature, quality and directions for IT education. We put together those important endeavours in the form of reports, statements and position papers. Such documents were of great historical significance for posterity.
- ***The Future Scenario***—IT education scene in India, at that moment, was built at the formal education level (comprising schools, colleges and universities) as well as the continuing education level (comprising the professional bodies, public organs, defence agencies and private organisation). It was important to project into the future in all these areas: to assess in which direction the IT education was heading for and whether such directions were appropriate. We attempted to make a foray into the future and offer recommendations that would appear feasible and sensible. Only the future, however, was to determine "the shape of things to come" in a Wellsian sense!

10

IT for Art and Culture (1991-94 and 2012 onwards)

The foray of IT into Indian art and culture was nothing short of spectacular in the 1990's. The organisation chosen to be the torch-bearer was the apex body, Indira Gandhi National Centre for the Arts (IGNCA) and the massive funding agent was none other than the United Nations Development Programmes (UNDP). Let me explain.

In the light of the connectivity between environment, development and culture, the need for creation of a facility that would use modern technology like IT to comprehend the unique and vast diversity of India's art heritage could not be over-emphasised. The latter should be disseminated, through appropriate networking: both within the country and outside. Through its programmes, besides heightening general awareness, an institution like IGNCA should be able to demonstrate that culture and development were not in confrontation and suggest how goals of development should be refined and redefined, taking cognizance of the quality of life with UNDP assistance. It should be possible to demonstrate how fragments of a cultural past could be reconstructed—at least virtually—so that not only the product, but the process as also the values underlying a cultural heritage were accessible to the currer t and future generations: in the modern language of technology.

Government of India—being conscious of the above enunciated role of culture and heritage in development—set up IGNCA in 1987: to look at art and development as central to all life. As an autonomous body, IGNCA was designated as a nodal agency to prescribe technical standards for all agencies under Central and State governments: for storage, retrieval and dissemination of data on arts, humanities and cultural heritage. IGNCA launched massive programmes for collecting multi-media (M-M) primary and secondary source materials by identifying thousands of repositories of unpublished manuscripts (MSS) in various institutions, libraries and museums and micro-filming of unpublished texts and images from MSS across the country.

IGNCA began functioning as a national resource centre for the arts to catalyse an integrated perception of Indian traditions and to stimulate awareness of our precious heritage among the following target beneficiaries :

- Planners and policy-makers at national and State levels;
- Scholars and researchers among social scientists, physical scientists, ecologists, ethnologists, archaeologists, archivists, art-historians, Indologists, etc.;
- Educators, teachers and students from formal and non-formal education streams;
- Tourists and tourism professionals from India and abroad;
- Designers, artisans and craftsmen; and
- Common people, tribal people, etc.

In the early 1990's, financial and intellectual investment in comprehensive documentation of scattered and fragmented heritage was not matched by outputs: due to lack of appropriate technology. This was also because of lack of suitable data models and encoding standards for developing M-M presentation in the field of art and culture, and due to lack of trained manpower to handle appropriate technology.

In 1991, I was selected to be the "National Project Director" under the inspiring guidance of Dr. Kapila Vatsyayan, during the project assistance (PA) phase for the project: "Strengthening National Facility for Interactive Multi-Media Documentation of Cultural resources", for which UNDP gave an initial input of $15,000, over 1991-92. I was assigned to prepare a systems analysis study,—to form the basis of the brief draft of the Project Formulation Framework (PFF). I also had the competent professional help of two National Project Coordinators—Dr. S.P. Mudur of National Centre of Software Technology (NCST), Mumbai and Dr. B.C. Kailay of NIC, Delhi—before submission of the more detailed document for UNDP approval in March 1992. The other international assistance was from UNESCO who chipped in to sponsor seminars in the broad area of culture and development.

Project Goals

The expected ends of our project were the following :

- IGNCA should be suitably strengthened—both in manpower and infrastructure—so as to fulfil its above mandate more effectively;
- There would be substantial jump in the rate of systematic and integrated documentation and dissemination of cultural resources;
- Data models and encoding standards would be available in the field of art and culture;
- Trained manpower would also be available, who would form the core group of professionals, in turn, training others;
- Linkages between IGNCA and other institutions would be strengthened and IGNCA would be enabled to effectively discharge its responsibilities as mandated; and
- IGNCA would be in a position to disseminate the processed information to the target beneficiaries in an effective manner.

Project Strategy

According to our project strategy, M-M technology was to allow the facility to integrate the three components of information: textual in ASCII code; visual and audio in binary code or digitalised form. While IGNCA had been set up as an apex body to promote holistic and integrated perception of cultural traditions of India, it was not meant to be a repository of objects embodying artistic and cultural creativity: whether they were in the textual, visual or audio form. What it sought to do was to provide a "forum" for making available to its users different trends and manifestations of Indian cultural legacy in an integrated way.

In other words, IGNCA was meant to bank upon a large number of national, cultural and educational institutions, like the National Library of India; National Archives of India; National Museum; Archaeological Survey of India; Sangeet Natak Akademi; National School of Drama; National Film Archive of India; Anthropological

Survey of India; Archives of AIR and DD; Central Institute of Educational technology; and other such institutions throughout the country (and abroad). IGNCA was to act as referral information facility. It was well nigh impossible to have such a networked and referral system operationalised, without the intervention of M-M technology and UNDP support that we sought was basically to accomplish this task.

Project Outcome (for Target Beneficiaries)

1. Audio-Visual (A.V.) documentation, reprographic material and publications to reach policy-makers, planners, environmentalists and others;
2. Digested, fully-processed material—through the A-V media, still images and exhibits of participatory workshops—to be made available to school students and teachers in both the formal and non-formal systems;
3. The analytical and syncretic tools of high technology to bring in a change in perception of scholars and researchers;
4. Appropriate visual and textual materials to be developed for dissemination to tourists and tourism operators;
5. AIR, DD and print media to be used to disseminate information for the common people; and
6. Training material to be developed and training courses organised by collaborating with key national institutions.

Project Success Criteria

Output 1—Interactive M-M facility in the field of art and culture.
Success Criteria—Operationalising M-M facility.

Input Activities

- Setting up of project management manpower;
- Study tours;
- Assessment of HW and SW;
- Selection of equipment;
- Creation of infrastructure;
- Procurement and installation of equipment;
- Testing on-site of installed items; and

- Setting up of systems management and maintenance manpower, etc.

Output 2—Training and consultancy capability in interactive M-M documentation.

Success Criteria—Standardised data models and encoding standards.

Input Activities

- Conceptual design of pilot projects;
- Source material identification and collection;
- Digitisation of source material;
- Detailed design and integration of captured material into M-M data-base;
- Design and creation of M-M presentation of pilot projects;
- Analysis of information content and structure of M-M documentation;
- Preparation of draft standard for M-M information, its distribution to art scholars and analysis of feed-back;
- Design, development and production of final report in interactive M-M;
- Refinement and validation of methodology of M-M applications;
- Training of 100 Indian scholars in use of M-M for art and culture; and
- Organisation of regional workshop for sharing information among neighbouring countries.

Output 3—Dissemination strategy, including training packages developed for target beneficiaries.

Success Criteria—Demand and acceptance of self-sustaining training programmes and benchmarks on impact.

Input Activities

- Identifying national institutions for different target beneficiaries;
- Networking and interacting with selected institutions;
- Planning and initiating training programmes and validating training material;

- Identifying select schools to inter-weave cultural and environmental dimensions into curriculum and analysis of feed-back;
- Chalking out enrichment strategy of primary school curriculum;
- Acting as an apex resource centre to sustain and expand such training;
- Devising mechanisms to monitor and assess impact of project activities on target beneficiaries; and
- Devising comprehensive strategy to disseminate results of various projects.

Our project document (PD) was finally accepted for the ensuing 5 years at UNDP's assistance level of $ 2.5 million and formally signed between UNDP on one side and Government of India (Department of Culture and Department of Economic Affairs) on the other side, in February 1994.

× × ×

An immediate follow-up of the UNDP project was to look at the potential applications for M-M in art and culture in the Indian sub-continent as follows:

1. Brahadishvara Temple at Thanjavur;
2. Cultural efflorescence around the twelfth century epic *Gita Govinda*;
3. Triveni area in Allahabad;
4. Puri Dham in Odisha around the Jagannath temple;
5. Brij Bhumi in the Uttar Pradesh;
6. Fatehpur Sikri in Agra (UP); and
7. Abounding sculpture of Avalokiteshvara Buddha.

Out of the seven, I was associated with the firsr two. For Brahdishvara Temple, I was sent to Thanjavur by Dr. Kapila Vatsyayan in the company of the eminent archaeologist Prof. Nagaswamy and marvelled at the multiple dimensions of that "temple of temples". It was a most accurately planned architectural wonder with the sanctum sanctorum and the frontally spread out segments of the temple laid in perfect proportions. Even its vertical spires took off in symmetric measures to the sanctum below. The sculptures—in relief or in grottos—were hewn in splendid style, with icons placed in the best traditions of iconography and iconometry prescribed in Indian *Shilpa Shastra*. There were marvellous paintings of the Shaivite saint poets on the inner walls in the form of narrative arts. If these were the aspects of visual arts, the performing arts were equally manifest in rituals and festivals through dance, music and chanting for each icon at each corner in space and spread—every year—over days, weeks and months in time.

[In February 1996, I presented an invited paper on "Usage of M-M in Art and Culture: Expectation, Application and Exploration" at the International Conference on "M-M Information System" organised by the IETE, with special reference to a fully-worked pilot project on Brahadishvara Temple in M-M form. However, 3-D graphics and archaeological "walk-through" were left out of my scope.]

For Jayadeva's *Gita Govinda*, I worked around at IGNCA with Ranjit Makkuni—from XEROX Paolo Alto Research Centre (PARC), USA—on his M-M video project on the immortal Sanskrit classic. Composed in the twelfth century in Bengal, it had 12-canto, 24-song text and had numerous commentaries arose all over the land from Odisha to Gujarat, from Nepal to Rajasthan. Sculpturally, the Radha-Krishna icons were the most prevalent since the medieval times when Jayadeva elevated Radha to the pedestal of divinity. Paintings on *Gita Govinda* were found in profusion all over India and were the most striking among the miniature paintings among the various schools of Rajasthan, Deccan and Pahadi. In performing arts, performances based on *Ashtapadis* (lyrics) from the epic provided the staple to all classical dances of India, and sung in Kerala temples.

[Both Brahadishvara Temple and the epic *Gita Govinda* were made into M-M projects by IGNCA later on, as seen below.]

× × ×

On the same lines as NIC was set up by DoE for operationalising UNDP assistance for IT in governance and administration in Central and State governments in 1977 (vide Chapter 3, "United Nations as 'Doubting Tom'), Cultural Informatics Laboratory (CIL) was set up by IGNCA for the UNDP assisted M-M documentation project in 1994. CIL has emerged as a world class documentation unit in IT domain that demonstrates the manner in which Indian heritage can be recreated "virtually", in the holistic and integrated perception of culture. The contents, developed by CIL serves as the end-point in the assembly-line of IGNCA's activities: presented to the world as thematic M-M through CD-ROMs, in-house KALASAMPADA (Digital Library—Resources of Indian Cultural Heritage) and the Website www.ignca.gov.in.

Some activities of CIL, under the benign leadership of Pratapanand Jha, are illustrated below in brief:

- **Kalasampada**—CIL acts as a focal point of digitisation of manuscripts, slides, books, audio and video: to preserve the entire repository of its present (and future) holdings in digital mode and to disseminate the cultural contents—in various digital formats—to scholars, researchers and the people in general. The facility is currently available in on "Intranet", as the IGNCA's archival collection is bound by intellectual property rights. The project is sponsored by Department of IT, Ministry of Communications and IT.
- **National Data-Bank on Indian Art & Culture**—IGNCA's visual archives include one lakh digital images (on various aspects of art and culture) and 1,000 hours of audio-video, with 25,000 rare books (from the ASI collection) to be uploaded on ASI Website and "walk-through" created of selected archaeological monuments and sites (like Humayun Tomb, Khajuraho, etc.).
- **Rock Art**—The twin programmes of "*Adi Drishya*" (primeval sight) and "*Adi Shravya*" (primeval sound) are based on Indian rock art—probably the oldest legacy of mankind—to become a user-friendly computer-aided learning (CAL) application for children.
- **Devadasi Murai**—This is a millennium old tradition in Tamil Nadu for good luck and well-being: created on a CD-ROM in 1997 to depict multi-dimensional performance by female ritual specialists within the architectural space of Brahadishvara temple.
- **Mukteshvara Temple**—A user-friendly interactive system allows the user to browse the multi-dimensional architectural, sculptural and inscriptional profile on the 11th - 12th century temple of Karnataka, where all facets of Indian civilisation—

encompassing religion, art and poetry—are exemplified with the highest degree of refinement.

- **Ajanta**—While many books, travelogues, films, photographs and collections exist on Ajanta, the present CD-ROM attempts to provide comprehensive view for students, teachers, tourists and scholars. It covers both periods of Ajanta: the Satavahana rules during the first century BC to first century AD when the Buddha was revered in the form of the stupa in the Theravada credo; and the Vakataka rules in the fifth century AD when the Buddha was revered in the human form in the Mahayana credo.
- **Brahadishvara Temple**—This project aims at a hyper-media presentation of an integrated view of the eleventh century Chola temple in Thanjavur (Tamil Nadu). It was still regarded as a "living" temple with traditions of ritual and performative practices alive within the temple-space resonating to its architecture and sculpture, painting and literature, and socio-economic structures, as investigated by a group of scholars.
- ***Gita Govinda***—A M-M experience of *Gita Govinda* was developed in order to familiarise audiences to the fundamental concepts of Indian music, dance, art and their inter-relationships in between December 1997 and January 1998. The experience comprised a network of 13 physical and virtual M-M spaces that reinterpreted 6 songs of the epic spatially, laid out across two circular rings. Arranged on the circular axis were the songs of the poem, showing various emotional situations of Radha and Krishna in amour. The two rings—representing the poem's meanings—attempted a major M-M documentation effort in video, audio, images and dance-movements involving, in total, 40 Gigabytes of authored *Gita Govinda* content.
- **Oral Epic of Devanarayana**—Devanarayana is a folk deity worshipped by the pastoral community of Gujjars in Rajasthan, where the 45-hour oral narrative contains both sung and spoken sections, performed in all the night vigils. The CD-OM is meant to focus on this oral tradition—painted on long scrolls—unfolding the story through singing and performance.
- **Two Pilgrims**—Paintings executed over 70 years by the twentieth-century Hungarian itinerant painters—Elizabeth

sass Brunner and Elizabeth Brunner, mother and daughter duo—are used to create a M-M data-base. While mother's paintings include Himalayan scenes, natural landscapes and symbolic constructions, the daughter's works concentrate on portraits of leaders and intellectuals, as well as nature and ancient Indian sculptures.

- **Agnichayana**—This inter-active content exploration system offers a highly complex structure of space-time coordinates, rituals, text and spoken word of Agnichayana: probably the oldest surviving ritual of humanity. It offers extraordinary insight into Vedic times; highlights the origin of many features of South Asian culture; and provides a unique opportunity for the study of oral tradition and transmission.
- **Vishvarupa**—This project aims at offering an interactive content exploration system to support study of Indian art, by offering a data-base of selected images of Vishvarupa Krishna: the cosmic vision of Krishna revealed to Arjuna in the *Bhagavad Gita*, tracing the root of Vishvarupa to the *Rigveda* onwards.
- **Man and Masks**—This is an interactive M-M presentation to support the study of masks—referring to the total personality of a person rather than an aspect of the self—by offering a data-base. It would use selected mask-images from IGNCA collection from 22 countries done in 1998.

Besides, CIL has been conducting digitisation projects of rare manuscripts in Oriental Research Library, Srinagar; 2,700 manuscripts in National Museum Delhi; many antiquities and 870 manuscripts of Tagore in Vishva-Bharati, Shantiniketan; 6,000 manuscripts, 1,500 sculptures and terracotta, and 1,000 paintings and coins in Allahabad Museum (UP); plus several other antiquities elsewhere in north and south India. Internationally, digitisation of Kanjuur and Danjuur manuscripts of Mongolia, Ulan Baatar, is a recent collaborative venture for CIL.

Today, CIL has powerful HW support by way of IBM LINUX server, 50 TB Fibre Optic storage system with duplicated interface power (expandable to 320 TB), Ethernet 100 GB, 10 Mbps Network Switcher, Router, Ethernet D-link, Ethernet Vivid,—with 28 work-stations /PCs and a whole host of peripherals for microfilm scanning, microfiche scanning, slide scanning, book (colour and B&W) scanning, digital camera, and video and audio digitisation stations.

× × ×

In a June 2011, study done on audio-visual (A-V) cultural archives, I observed that India's immensely rich A-V cultural resources provide "intangible cultural heritage", comprising basically *audio* (chants, recitations, music, interviews, speeches and audio component of composite media) and video (films, documentaries, video-recording of events, festivals, life-style studies, ritual documentation, performing arts of theatre, dance, puppetry, mime, etc., and video component of composite media). Between the twin media of A-V, they hold the enormous power to provide recordings for all plastic, graphic, visual and performing arts !

Alongside the flourishing of human civilisation, the felt need for the media and the growth of modern recording technology,—I noted that there have been essentially two media formats: *Analog* (with continuous and unbroken recording) and *Digital* (with discrete recording on binary '0-1' base, making it amenable to computer processing). Obviously, *Digital* technology has total advantage over the *Analog*, making possible the following:

1. Near-permanent durability,
2. Need-based quality enhancement,
3. Highly economic digital storage, and
4. Almost instant retrieval.

Globally, the evolution of media formats has seen a highly skewed development. In general, the available *audio media* formats of *Analog* kind are as follows :

1.Phonographic cylinder, 2. Music roll, 3. Gramophone record, 4. Wire recording, 5. Electrical cut record, 6. Magnetic record, 7. Electrical transcription, 8. Vinyl record, 9.Stereophonic vinyl record, 10. 4-track stereo, 11. Compact cassette, 12. 8-track stereo, 13. Micro cassette, 14. Mini cassette, 15. Quad 8-track, 16. Quad vinyl record.

Available *audio media* formats of *Digital* kind are as follows :

1. Betamax digital audio, 2. Eleaset, 3. Digital laser disc, 4. Compact disc (CD), 5. High-definition CD, 6. Digital audio tape (DAT), 7. Mini disc, 8. Digital compact cassette, 9. DVD, 10. DTS-CD, 11. DVD-Audio, 12. Super audio CD, 13. Dual disc, 14. HD DVD, 15. Blu-Ray, 16. Slot music.

Available *video media* formats of *Analog* kind are as follows:

1. 1" video tape (Bosch), 2. 1" video tape (Ampex-Sony), 3. 2" video tape (Ampex), 4. Ampex, 5. Betacam, 6. Betacam SP, 7. Betacam (Sony), 8. S-VHS (JVC), 9. U-matic (Sony), 10. VCR, 11. VCR-LP, 12. SVR, 13. VERA, 14. VHS (JVC), 15. VHS-C (JVC), 16. Video 2000 (Philops).

Available *video media* formats of *Digital* kind (including optical storage) are:

1.Betacam IMX (Sony), 2. D-VHS (JVC), 3. D-Theatre, 4. D1 (Sony), 5. D2 (Sony), 6. D3 (Sony), 7. D5 (Sony), 8. D9 (JVC), 9. Digital betacam (Sony), 10. Digital 8 (Sony), 11. DVC, 12. DVD, 13. UMD (Sony), 14. HDV. 15. ProHD (JVC), 16. MicroMV, 17.Mini DV.

× × ×

Since IGNCA is India's foremost national resource centre for multiple forms of art and culture, I proposed in June 2011 to evolve a comprehensive model for IGNCA's own A-V cultural archive. My proposal, as recommended by IGNCA, was accepted by the Ministry of Culture under the newly-initiated "Tagore National Fellow" scheme and I was selected as "Tagore Research Scholar" for this project at IGNCA for 2 years from June 2012 onwards.

At a rough guess, IGNCA's A-V resources cover some 4,000 hours: distributed internally among its Cultural Archive, Media Centre and other holding divisions like Kalakosha, Kalanidhi and Janapada Sampada. Broadly, they fall under the following general categories:

- **Interview**—Such as, "Great Masters Series" comprising, *inter alias*, 23 illuminating interviews by Dr. Kapila Vatsayan of luminaries like Zohra Segal, Mulk Raj Anand, Sitara Devi, Sumati Mutatkar, Premlata Sharma, Maya Rao and others.

- **Ritual Documentation**—Such as, Naga Mandala in South Karnataka, Abthoryam Yajna in Kerala, Naba Kalebara ritual of Puri Jagannath, Sacred World of the Todas in the Nilgiris, Lai Haraoba ritual dance of Maitis in Manipur, Mudiyatam ritual dance of Kerala.
- **Archaeological Site and walk-through**—Such as, "Speaking Rocks" of Badami caves.
- **Events**—Such as, Braj Mahotsava, Masked Dances of Hemis festival in Ladakh.
- **Festivals**—Such as, Mahamastaka Abhishekam in Karkela, Wangale Gara festival, Soz on Martyrdom of Imam Hussain, Bidesia by Bhikari Thakur, Maharas of Manipur, Tamasha of Maharashtra and Rajasthan, Karkha of Khwaja Moinuddin Chisti, Pandavani by Teejan Bai on *Mahabharata*,
- **Performing Arts : Dance**—Such as, Ammanur Madhav Chakiyar's several *Vesham* and *Kriyas*, Acharya Parvati Kumar's depiction of *Abhinaya Darpana* in Bhratanatyam, Kalyani Kutty *Amma's Mohiniyatam* recital, *Kudiyattam* of Kerala, *Gita Govinda* by Rukmini Devi Arundale in Bharatanatyam and Amobi Singh in Manipuri.
- **Performing Arts : Music**—Such as, Pt. L.K. *Pandit's Gwalior Gharana* music, S, Krishnaswamy's collection of 30 hours of Carnatic music, A.K. Ranga Rao's collection of 740 Carnatic music concerts, S. Natarajan's collection of Carnatic music concerts from 1955 onwards, music performances and teaching techniques of Maniyakkama Saride, T. Brinda and others.
- **Performing Arts : Theatre**—Such as, *Panchatantra* in puppetry by LBT, Gwalior, Surabhi Theatre of Andhra, the Bhramyaman Kahinoor Theatre of Assam, Radha's *Man Bhanjana* in *Ras Lila* of Braj.
- **Lectures**—Such as, talks on Suniti Kumar Chattopadhyay, "Music in Indian Art" by Vidya Niwas Mishra.
- **Seminars**—Such as, "*Kala*" on concept of time, "*Kham*" on space, "*Dhwani*" on sound, "*Prakriti*" on Nature, "*Akara*" on alphabet and calligraphy.
- **Workshop**—Such as, "Conservation".
- **Films**—Such as, acquired films of Joseph Campbell, Debes Bhattacharya, etc.

Project Step One—Digitisation

It is understood that Media Centre has done a commendable job of digitisation already and Cultural Archive is to take up digitisation shortly. All of the selected materials should be digitised in-house or preferably outsourced to vendors who specialise in round-the-clock digitisation process.

Project Step Two—Documentation

Experts need be familiar with "metadata" that covers cataloguing and indexing for on-line use. "Metadata" is data on data, as value-added information that would be used to arrange, describe, track and otherwise enhance access to IGNCA's A-V material;, pave a standard way to describe network-accessible materials; enable precise queries to be made by user-scholars and researchers; and help search-engines present "hits": grouped by subjects and key-words, rather than in a random mode.

The above requires metadata input formats (called "data-sheets") to be devised with sufficient care to create key-words from the beginning (and vetted by subject-area experts from whom feed-back should be obtained to correct the key-words), so that the data-sheets can thereafter be filled up by trained metadata assistants. Data-sheets should be standardised and made globally compatible by use of the international standard data-elements of "Dublin Core Metadata Element Sets" (DCMES, vide full details in Chapter 12, "Interactive Website for Indian Icons").

DCMES is meant for ordinary users to formulate a descriptive record-base in an easily-understood scheme and offers relatively simple format: with international support and is universally recognised. Focussed attention in DCMES is given to the following :

- *Technical details* regarding *content* (source, subject/keywords, title, type, scope/coverage, description/abstract, relation);
- *Administrative details* regarding *intellectual property* (contributor, creator, publisher, copyright); and
- *House-keeping details* regarding *Version* (date, format, identifier, language).

Project Step Three—Keywords

"Groups of keywords"—within a controlled vocabulary—should be identified, to comprise "main keywords/ key-phrases" and "sub-keywords": under the overall ambit of "Library of Congress Subject Holding" (LCSH) for ease of identification even in the global context. "Thesaurus", if necessary, should be created for smooth identification of subjects and areas in terms of synonyms and related words.

Project Step Four—Ingestion

Once metadata are created on-line from the DCMES-friendly data-sheets — using the prescribed "keywords"—by the metadata assistants for digitised records and evaluated thereafter for any correction, they should be "ingested" by CIL with their in-house SW. This is the stage of hyper linking of the keywords to the main materials: for inter-active access and retrieval of the latter by scholars and researchers on the IGNCA "Intranet" in the public domain to provide a referral service within the IGNCA complex.

How much and how far the ingested materials should be put on the IGNCA Website is a matter of later policy decision, but the project from Step One to Step Four should be easily replicable—subject only to IGNCA sharing its Ingesting SW for on-line access and retrieval on the respective Intranets—for very rich A-V cultural archives belonging to the following nationally-important organisations, with whom I have held a preliminary dialogue:

1. Sangeet Natak Akdemi, Delhi,
2. National School of Drama, Delhi, and
3. National Centre for Performing Arts, Mumbai.

My project as "Tagore Research Scholar" at IGNCA is due to be completed in June 2014.

11

Foray into China with IT (2001-03)

In early 2001 and again in early 2002, two of mainland China's inter-university delegations visited Indian institutions and organisations to work out academic collaborations. When they came to visit XANSA (India) complex in Delhi and NOIDA, they looked with some interest at my two academic involvements of teaching full 30-hour courses on "Management Strategy for Information Technology": at IMI, Delhi, for teaching MBA students (Final Year, seconded from Industry) in 1999 and 2000; and at JNU, Delhi, for teaching MCA (Final Year) in 2001.

Among outcomes of their visits were kind invitations extended to me to teach in some of the premiere universities in mainland China as follows:

May-June, 2002

- Beijing University of Aeronautics and Astronautics, Beijing;
- Dalian University of Technology, Dalian;
- Jiao Tong University, Shanghai; and
- South-East University, Nanjing.

I conducted Guest Lecture Series to Under-Graduate and Post-Graduate students of Computer Science and Management (Final Year).

September-October, 2002

- Bayhang University, Beijing—Two 30-hour courses for full-time and part-time PG students (Final Year);
- Tsing Hua University, Beijing—One 12-hour course for PG students (Final Year); and
- South-East University, Nanjing—Two 30-hour courses for full-time and part-time PG students (Final Year);

All courses were conducted in their respective Schools of Software Engineering.

September, 2003

- Yunan University, Kunming (old and new campuses)—two 30-hour courses for PG students (Final Year), in the School of Software Technology.

All course-participants in every institute were evaluated, based on objective tests and were given credits accordingly.

The professors and academicians of these universities, who coordinated all academic matters, organised examinations and evaluations, and arranged generous hospitality for me in University hotels and plush guest-houses, included the following:

1. *Tsinghua University, Beijing* —
   Prof Lin Qiang, Asst. Dean, School of Software;
2. *Bayhang University* (Name changed from *Aeronautics* and *Astronautics), Beijing* —
   Prof Yao Shushen, Dy. Dean, Computer Science and Engineering;
   Prof. Jingnong Wen, Technical Director, UNIWARE Co. Ltd.;
3. *South-East University, Nanjing* —
   Prof. Michael Y. Qu, Department of Computer Science and Engineering;
   Prof. Yeuquan Wu, College of Software Engineering;
4. *Jiao Tong University, Shanghai* —
   Prof Yuxi Fu, Department of Computer Science;
   Prof Chen Yue, Division of International Cooperation and Exchange;

5. *Dalian University of Technology, Dalian* —
   Prof. Xue Qiang, Deputy Head, School of Computer Software;
6. *Yunan University, Kunming* —
   Prof. Wangshi Pu, Chair, School of Software;
   Prof. Li Tong, Vice Dean, School of Software.

Each 30-hour course—materials circulated in advance through CDs and printed booklets, in addition to students making copies of POWERPOINT presentations through pen-drives—covered the following 2-hour lectures each:

Management Choice

- Management Choice of Hardware Technology;
- Management Choice of Software technology; and
- Management Choice of Communications Technology.

Technology Review

- Management of Client-Server Technology;
- Management Use of Data Warehouse and Data Mining;
- Management of On line Integrated Systems; and
- National Resource Management with Satellite Technology.

Managing Enterprises

- e-commerce and Electronic Data Exchange (EDI); and
- Enterprise resource Planning and Business Process Re-engineering (BPR).

Management Strategy

- IT Planning Strategy: An Industry Experience; and
- IT as a Business Strategy Tool.

Wider Management Environment

- Executive Computing: Planning and Support;
- Business Process Outsourcing (BPO): IT in Public Service;
- e-governance: From Policy to Practice; and

- ISO-9000, Six Sigma, Capability Maturity Model: Indian Experience.

The goals at the end of the above, highly practice-oriented, course were consciously made out to be as follows:

1. Judging self-knowledge by going through structured objective tests;
2. Using IT in working life: productively and purposively: in diverse management applications; and
3. Achieving better rapport among the IT and Management disciplines and reduce communication gap to a substantial extent.

× × ×

During my three lecture-trips on IT, as above, to six major universities in Beijing, Dalian—a lovely harbour-city on the Yellow Sea—Shanghai, Kunming and Nanjing, many fascinating facts came to light for me. Let me record them.

First, the "Internet" usage in China was hobbled by prohibitive costs of personal computers (PCs). The average "comrade" in a city had to work for almost two years before he could afford to buy a Made-in-China PC, at his current level of income. The available brands from Samsung and Hyundai—for PENTIUM 4, Network adapter, video-adapter and wide screen—were priced at nearly $1,000 and laptops from IBM and DELL went beyond $1,200. There was a large enough base of assembled products that were a little less costly,—but all these had high prices compared to the available income-bracket.

Second, the government in Beijing was no doubt pinning its hope on high technology and the Internet was viewed as a means of catapulting China into the future. On the flip side, however, the "Falun Gong" group—who had surrounded once the Communist Party (CP) leadership at their Beijing precincts to voice its protests—had organised themselves over the Internet. Branded as "an evil cult" and outlawed, the group was armed only with one another's e-mail addresses!

Third, while the Internet was based on free availability and widespread diversity, the notions that underpinned the political China were CP's monopoly. Mao Dze Dong, after all, built his China upon the concept of self-sufficiency, which ultimately implied isolation. But the monopoly over information was not easy in an electronic age. Even through all the phone-lines of foreigners in Shanghai city might or might not be monitored earlier, it was increasingly difficult for Beijing to monitor every Website. Attempts had been made though, such as, CP Bureau for the Protection of State Secrets using comprehensive Internet regulations in January 2000, or, China's strict encryption registration requirements, issued immediately thereafter. "But these vague and sweeping rules lie in wait for unsuspecting victims in the future", as someone observed to me, noting that the dictum of China's Public Security Bureau was: In order to inspect the Internet, one must control it.

Finally, while Beijing had opted to open up the country to the Internet in the early 1990's, some higher-ups were already having second thoughts. Jiang Mianheng, the US-educated engineer son of President Jiang Zenin, had proposed that China must build a national network that was independent of the Internet. According to him, the Chinese Net (C-Net) would be in the Chinese language, run on locally developed chips and protocols, and would have local contents supporting CP's message. But with C-Net, did Beijing try to cut off China from the rest of the world ?

If the IT climate in the universities was any indication, this did not seem to be so. In 2001-02, there were 1065 universities across China (compared to India's just over 200 at that time) and, out of them, the top 100 universities held the pride of place for research and study. There was a fierce competition every year among 2 million students for seats in these universities. Called GAO KAO and held in the form of a 3-day examination in June (dreaded as "Black June" by the candidates!), only 1 out of 8 got admission to these 100 universities, Only 1 out of 20 could go to the top 10, from which, incidentally, modern China's leadership hailed. These *crème de la crème* institutions were: Tching Hua University (Beijing), Peking University, Shanghai Jia Tong University (from which came the Chinese President), Zhe Jiang University, Nanjing University, Fu Dan University (Nanjing), Harbin Industrial University, Nan Kai University (Tian Jing), Tian Jing University and Tiang Ji University (Shanghai). All of them were "happy hunting grounds" for IT, where all students had access to the Internet and possessed their own global e-mail addresses.

Looking closely at the IT scene, I could not fail to notice the exalted status hardware had in China. Every university teaching science and technology had a department of hardware research and maintenance,—so that, among other things, the country's population of assembled PCs was well looked after. The chip and component manufacturing giants, Founder Corporation and Legend Corporation—headquartered in Beijing—dwarfed any hardware facility that India had ever created. Universities had so far taught diligently computer science subjects, as a result of which the fundamental principles and concepts were very well rooted. Now they were looking at the software engineering area, which—in the absence of scientific applications in the industrial practice—was not so well looked after. In order to make up for the lost time, as many as 35 software institutions were opened within 2002,—taking a long leap into the future. One of the immediate end-users would be the Science and Technology Committee for the 2008 World Olympics, which had the responsibility for construction of the stadiums, developing Olympic Information System, and planning the opening and closing ceremonies.

Modern China was looking askance at modern India and seemed keen to join hands in the IT domain. For one, India was still relatively strong in software engineering, which was fully recognised in the Chinese IT circle. With an early start, efficient legal safeguards and overwhelming advantage in English language, India had stolen a march over many other nations. This was evidenced by the fact that India had 16 software companies certified by Carnegie-Melon University's Software Engineering Institute (SEI) at "Level 5", the highest for Capability Maturity Model (CMM),—out of a global total of 50 or so. In sharp contrast, China had only one CMM "Level 3" company and was keen to reduce the handicap. For another, India had proven capability in software project management and delivering products on-site abroad. China wished to learn these skills and indeed, other skills to capture "outsourcing" of IT services by the multi-national giants, where India had been catering to more than one-third of the "Fortune 500" companies. Another potential area was the application software packages built around the LINUX operating system. The LINUX user-groups at Mumbai and Bangaluru could work with their counterparts in Beijing and Shanghai. On the whole, the hardware strength of China could certainly have hand-holding with the software strength of India: to achieve an "Asian Miracle".

12

Interactive Website for National Icons (2008-09)

India's cultural heritage—spanning millennia—was spread over the length and breadth of the country, although a lot of the material had migrated overseas over time. Leaving out books —whose number is a legion—the legacy, in the form of *primary* materials, extended from architecture and sculpture spread over the entire country up to paintings, photographs, puppets, artifacts and manuscripts held closely by individuals in their private collections.

Speaking of *secondary* material—namely, not the actual legacy that can be touched and felt, but their records kept in the archives of our land—such archival records could be broadly of three kinds of media:

- *Moving Image*—Film, video and animation, recording any actual or imaginary event, story, documentary, performance, interview, fair, festival, "walk-through" of architectural sites, etc.;
- *Still Images*—Graphics (painting, photograph, etching), microfilm, microfiche, manuscripts, books, etc.; and
- *Sound*—Audio recording of music, chanting, elocution, etc.

Alongside the flourishing of civilisation, the felt need for the media and the growth of modern recording technology,— there had been essentially two media-formats: *Analog* (with continuous and unbroken recording) and *Digital* (with discrete recording in the form of '0-1', making it amenable to computer processing). *Digital* technology has immense advantage over the *Analog*, making possible the following (vide Chapter 10, "IT for Art and Culture"):

1. Near-permanent durability;
2. Need-based quality enhancement;
3. Highly economic storage;
4. Very fast information transfer; and
5. Almost instant retrieval.

× × ×

At the turn of the new century from 2001 to 2006, one of my major concerns was to explore the following :

- Whether the country's premiere audio-visual (A-V) archives could be persuaded to convert their *Analog* materials into standard *Digital* resources;
- Simultaneously, if they could be urged to create cataloguing and indexing data for their *Digital* records; and
- Whether the cataloguing and indexing data could be of international compatibility and amenable to global exchange.

If digitisation was important for value-addition to the A-V records, tagging (or "ingesting") of cataloguing data would be of equally crucial importance, for, the digital records were made for an "invisible cultural heritage" and not amenable to visual identification. In any case, the situation would be much like visiting a vast library and look into what would be an ocean of books, if there were no catalogue and index !

With the above two objectives, my exploratory visits in the early 2000s included the following cultural archives holding incredibly rich A-V records :

1. IGNCA, Delhi—meeting the Academic Director, Prof. Indranath Choudhuri;
2. Samudri Foundation, Chennai—meeting the Director, Pattavi Raman;
3. National Centre of Performing Arts (NCPA), Mumbai—meeting Chairperson, Vijaya Mehta;
4. Sangeet-Natak Akademi, Delhi—meeting the Secretary, Jayant Kastuvar;

5. National Gallery of Modern Arts, Delhi—meeting the Director, Rajeev Lochan;
6. National School of Drama, Delhi—meeting the Chairperson, Amal Allana;
7. Archaeological Survey of India, Delhi—meeting the Director General;
8. National Museum, Delhi—meeting the Director General; and
9. Asiatic Society of India, Kolkata—meeting the General Secretary.

Besides, I met the then Education Secretary, Government of India and Regional Representative, UNESCO. While, without exception, they—all highly motivated officials—confirmed nil-to-mediocre progress in digitisation of cultural records, nearly none professed involvement in tagging on any globally compatible indexing system for the A-V records. [I also sent e-mails on the subject to my mentor, Sam Pitroda, who responded by asking me to get in touch with DG of NIC, V.K. Gairola.]

In March 2008, I was intimated about my selection as "Chief Coordinator" for the "Leaders of India Project" (earlier named "Mahatma Project"), as conveyed from Dr. Gairola through Kamalini Dutt, the dynamic Director of D.D. Archives. The Project-idea was apparently suggested at the highest level in the Government of India and the CEO of Prasar Bharati, JS Lalli, announced that the Project would cover four of the iconic leaders of our nation :

- Mahatma Gandhi,
- Pt. Jawaharlal Nehru,
- Indira Gandhi, and
- Rajiv Gandhi.

The Project's goal was laid out to be the creation of an interactive Website on the A-V holdings—collected from all over the world—for these four top leaders: to be accessible from anywhere on the globe. [Later, when a prototype was shown to the Central Minister, Jairam Ramesh in his chamber, the latter suggested extension of the Project to some more iconic leaders and named them, but the suggestion was seemingly put on hold, although some preliminary work was done by us.]

Preliminaries

Before we began, we thought it would be desirable to check how other iconic global leaders—like Presidents of the USA and Prime Ministers of the UK—were presented on the world's Websites. Searching "Google" and "Yahoo!", among others we found that their biographical profiles (and some pictures) provided summary of their lectures: under headings like political aspects, economic aspects, social aspects, education aspects and international aspects. These materials were mostly run in a linear fashion, but were not interactive.

Since our idea was to make our Website inter-active, we wanted to provide the following additional facilities:

1. "Simple search" by curious onlookers through casual browsing of the running material, and "advanced search" by interested scholars and researchers, accessing the audio and video text/profile: armed with relevant keywords/key phrases;
2. Provision of a controlled vocabulary of keywords/key-phrases which could be used for "advanced search";
3. Presentation of each audio and video text/profile as divided into convenient "clippings" of 2-3 minutes each with "time-coding from" and "time-coding to" through "non-linear editing", and each "clipping" amenable to "advanced search" by relevant keywords/key-phrases; and
4. Preparation of a "thesaurus" with English and Hindi equivalents of keywords/key-phrases so that a bi-lingual "advanced search" was feasible.

Qualitatively, such a Website would perhaps be considered ahead of their foreign counterparts in "advanced search" facilities !

First Step

We set out to collect A-V material on the four great leaders by nationally and internationally advertising in the mass media. At the same time, an inter-disciplinary team was set up—with the involvement of Doordarshan (DD) Archives and All India Radio (AIR) Archives—to scour through the A-V materials collected at computer terminals in the "pre-view" rooms of DD and AIR.

Keeping in view the very large amount of A-V holdings available throughout the world—including BBC, CNN and many interested foreign photo-journalists of Indian and foreign origin—and remembering that there was a time-bound completion-target set for us, we decided to concentrate on 100 hours each of video and 100 hours each of audio on each of the top leaders, collected, *inter alia*, as follows:

- ***Mahatma Gandhi***—Largely from Zhaveri Collections, most assiduously gathered throughout Mahatma's life,—subject to copyright. AIR had most amazing audios on Mahatma's last few prayer-meetings.
- ***Jawaharlal Nehru***—Very well-covered by Films Division of India, DD and AIR, Nehru Memorial Museum and Library (NMML), and Nehru Memorial Fund.
- ***Indira Gandhi***—Besides Films Division of India, DD and AIR, materials came from Indira Gandhi Memorial Trust as well as from NMML.
- ***Rajiv Gandhi***—Besides Films Division of India, DD and AIR, valuable materials were available from Rajiv Gandhi Foundation.

Second Step

We decided to prepare the "streaming" text alongside the transmitted A-V footage for the Website. Accordingly, we requested colleagues to listen to each tape: "clipping" by "clipping", and asked them to write them down, on-line. In order to make sure of the authenticity of the A-V text, so recorded, that could finally run side by side. Subject-area experts were requested to "pre-view" each tape, again clipping by clipping, and "audit" each clipping and ultimately, the full tape. The text-format headings could be illustrated as follows :

Tape No. : XXX/ DVC—YY/ZZ
WWW/ DIGI-BETA /AA/BB

Programme : Indira —Presentation of U-Thant Award to Smt. Gandhi (example)

Reading : 00:34—00:25: 34

Duration : 23 mts. 00 sec.
Source : Doordarshan
Prasar Bharati.

The actual recording was made under five headings, namely, Sr No.; Time-Code Reading (clipping from—clipping to); Text (full text in that clipping); Keywords-Key-phrases; Group No.

Third Step

Keeping in view the aspect of international compatibility, subject-area experts evolved the final "controlled vocabulary" of keywords/key-phrases (with codes) for audio and video, as follows, to be marked on each "clipping" by use of "time-coding in" and "time-coding out":

01—BIOGRAPHY—(Description) Reference to personal details; achievements; milestones; happenings (e.g., childhood, education, career, marriage, family relationships, including parents, wife, children);

02—DATE, EVENT, LOCATION—(Description) The particular date on which the event occurred, speech was delivered, etc.;

03—PEOPLE, PLACES, THINGS—(Description) References to Persons, Organisations, Places and Things/Objects made in the actual event or during speech;

04—POLITICAL ISSUES—(Description) Independence/Freedom, Partition, Refugees, Terrorism, Constitutional Amendments, Legislations, National Security, Nuclear Arms, Disarmament, Fast, Imprisonment, Mass Movement, Popular Resistance, Civil Disobedience, Defence;

05—ECONOMIC ISSUES—(Description) Industry (including Cottage Industry), Machinery, Growth, Self-reliance, Poverty, Production, Planning, Export, Trade, Commerce, Banks, Money-related issues, Khadi, Charkha;

06—SOCIAL ISSUES—(Spiritual, Moral, Religious, Cultural, Societal)—(Description) Moral, Religion, Spirituality, Philosophy, Caste, Faith, Untouchability, Social Evils, Women/Children, Literature, Art, Music, Media, Reservation, Police, Social Policies, Social Reforms, Villages, Rural/Urban Society;

07—DEVELOPMENT ISSUES (Environment, Education, Science & Technology, Youth, Sports)—(Description) Health,

Science, Technology, Space, Education, Environment, Sports, Youth, Energy, Petroleum, Oil, Atomic/Nuclear Energy, Village Development;

08—INTERNATIONAL ISSUES—(Description) UN, Treaties, Agreements, Summits (NAM, CHOGM, WHO, FAO, WTO, UNESCO, UNDO, UNIDA, ESCAP, SAARC, IMF, ADB, WB), Foreign Visits, Foreign Policy;

09—QUOTES & SPEECHES—(Description) Quotations and Speeches given/delivered by the leaders.

Fourth Step

Keywords/key-phrases (with Codes) for audio and video had the following "Thesaurus" (with Devnagari Script, indicated in italics) to allow for synonymous searches:

01—BIOGRAPHY—*Jeevanvritt*
02—DATE, EVENT, LOCATION—*Tithi, Awasar/Ghatna, Sthal*
03—PEOPLE, PLACES, THINGS—*Vyakti, Sthan, Vastuyen*
04—POLITICAL ISSUES—*Rajnaitik Mudde*
05—ECONOMIC ISSUES—*Arthik Mudde*
06—SOCIAL ISSUES (Spiritual, Moral, Religious, Cultural, Social)—*Samajik Mudde (Adhyatmik, Naitik, Dharmik, Sanskritik, Samajik)*
07—DEVELOPMENT ISSUES (Environment, Education, Science & Technology, Youth, Sports)—*Vikasparak Mudde (Paryavaran, Shiksha, Vigyan aur Takniki, Yuva, Khel)*
08—INTERNATIONAL ISSUES—*Antarrashtriya Mudde*
09—QUOTES & SPEECHES—*Kathan / Bhashsan / Udgar.*

Fifth Step

Keywords/key-phrases were "ingested" with the audio and video materials—fully time-coded and "clippings" marked accordingly—through appropriate SW (DALET Asset Manager from HCL) and loaded on the DD server installed under "Media Asset management" (MAM, see below).The work done was double-checked and the running texts and keywords/key-phrases' tagging were evaluated from the quality viewpoint.

Sixth Step

A unique feature added was the "time-lines", i.e., dated listing of crucial biographical events in the life of these great leaders, such as, "Fasts", "Satyagrahas", "Jail-Yatra" in Mahatma's life; "Jail-Yatra" in Nehru's life, etc.

Final Step

Actual creation of the interactive Website—based on the "ingested" audio and video material, with clippings duly tagged with keywords/key-phrases—was outsourced to M/s Prime-Focus, based in India and the UK. After designing, testing and evaluating the materials, the "Leaders of India" assets were transferred to the NIC server, as per contracts.

To our entire satisfaction, the interactive Website was launched—under the name of www.leadersofindia.gov.in—in October 2010. [The actual arrangement of promoting the Website and its possible extension to other iconic national leaders lay in the official domain and hopefully would be resolved soon.]

× × ×

Aided by some little assistance from me (including an earlier orientation-seminar on "Digitisation of Cultural Archives" at Prasar Bharati under the then CEA'a invitation and subsequent dialogues with DD Archives on meta-data management and Dublin Core Meta-data Element Set, see below)), the DD Archives took up the massive task of digitisation of all its contents: collected and preserved in its regional libraries across the country. It was a rich visual history of India's recent past of 40 years, as the Public Service Broadcast had not left any aspect of this country untouched.

Such a "media asset" was a great treasure and was planned to be converted into "virtual archive" through a high-end Media Asset Management (MAM) solution. Thanks to the initiative of Kamalini Dutt, Director, DD Archives acquired the solution in November 2008. MAM was to preserve the Archive's treasure for posterity and also to enable its easy retrieval. In the one year till November 2009, old DD professionals—having the institutional memory of the contents created earlier—were actively involved in building the "virtual archive". The cardinal feature of this archive was its "Meta-data" tagging.

As mentioned in Chapter 10, "Meta-data" was the name given to the systematic information on cataloguing and indexing, discussed there. It could be viewed as follows:

- Value-added information that IT professionals created to arrange, describe, track and otherwise enhance access to primary materials: as information objects;
- Providing a standard way to describe network-accessible materials;
- Enabling precise queries to be made;
- Helping search-engines to present "hits" grouped by subjects (rather than a random mix);
- Meant for ordinary users to formulate descriptive records, based on a simple scheme.

Among International standards, Dublin Core Meta-data Element Set (DCMES) was a standard—arrived at by IT professionals and library scientists together at Dublin, Ohio, and globally accepted as well as maintained—widely used to describe digital materials, such as, video, sound, image, text and composite media like Web pages. In fact, DCMES, as a standard, was meant for cross-domain information resource description and included two levels: *Simple* and *Qualified.*

Simple DCMES was meant for broadcasting archive, sound archive, moving image archive and photograph archive, among others. It had 15 elements:

Content (Technical Details)

- Source—Source of derivation;
- Subject—name;
- Keywords/Key-phrases (Discussed earlier), derived from Library of Congress Subject-Holdings (LCSH), Library of Congress Catalogues (LCC), Dewey Decimal Catalogues (DDC), Universal Decimal Catalogues (UDC), etc.;
- Title—name;
- Type—name of the genre;

- Coverage—Extent, sequence;
- Description—Abstract;
- Relation—Reference to a relation.

Intellectual Property (Administrative Details)

- Contributor—Director;
- Creator—Author, Playwright;
- Publisher—Archivist; and
- Rights—IPR, copyright.

Version (House-keeping Details)

- Date—Event in the performance-cycle;
- Format—Physical, digital;
- Identifier—ISBN, ISSN; and
- Language—For intellectual content.

Qualified *DCMES included three additional elements, namely,*

- Audience;
- Provenance;
- Rights-holder.

This also included a group of element refinements: to refine the semantics of the elements that might be useful in finding resource.

On the whole, DCMES had the following advantages:

1. Suitable general approach (for library, archives, Web-technology communities) for standardisation of meta-data;
2. Relatively simple format, extendable into local fields;
3. International support (Radio broadcasting, sound, moving images, photographs, etc., archives);
4. Helpful to users to locate features;
5. Widely recognised and supported;
6. Used directly in Websites and as records in databases because of the way it was structured;
7. Maintained in a stable environment; and
8. Continuing development assured.

In DD Archives, DBMES formats used were carefully evolved into the following nine types:

- Performing Arts—Music, Dance, Theatre;
- Film;
- Documentary;
- Fine / Visual Arts;
- Allied Performing Arts—Animation, Mime, Puppetry, Ventriloquism;
- Crafts;
- Communications;
- Variety programmes; and
- Events—live / recorded.

We found DD Archive's DBMES formats—meant for MAM—as eminently satisfactory in their evaluation session in December 2008.

IT Overview

In today's world of technology, it still took nearly 100 years for telephones to reach 50 million users; 30 years for television; but only 5 years for the Internet. By 2001, the Internet-users in China alone reached a staggering figure of 22.5 million;—more than double that of 2000. In a land of great hopes and aspirations like China, there are multiple users per Internet account—as was the case in India. In fact, at the current growth-rates, it is estimated that the number of "Netizens" in China would surpass that of the USA by the year 2015. What is more, by the year 2015, the Chinese would be the most commonly used language on the Internet! Would Hindi also aspire to have a remotely second comparable popularity?

Leaving such speculations aside, we wish to look globally at some of the crucial IT issues that are emerging at the turn of the millennium. [What follows are, inter *alia*, jottings from my "View-port" column in *Computers Today* and my "Science" column in *The Statesman*].

Band-width

Specifically at 2001-02, India had a pathetic 325 Megabits per second (Mbps). China, as a late entrant then, had already notched 55 Gbps, the UK had 12 Gbps; Japan 160 Gbps; and USA 500 Gbps. As though it were not enough, the USA galloped towards vBNS (very High Performance Backbone Network Service), a project of MCI Telecommunications and National Science Foundation (NSF)—slated to achieve a few Terabits per second (Tbps). Like the old NSFnet, vBNS has been an American national network supporting the academic and research community of 120 universities and 25 corporate sponsors in the Internet-2. The latter has given the bandwidth of 2.4 Gigabits to each of the 77 institutions already.

Dovetailed with vBNS was also the US Federal Government initiative of New Generation Internet (NGI) which the White House had promoted to remove road-blocks for continued American dominance in technology innovation. NGI's goal was "to research, develop and experiment with advanced network technologies that will provide dependability, diversity, security and real-time capability for such applications as wide-area distributed computing, tele-operations and remote control of experimental facilities". NGI's goal two was the actual networking, depending heavily upon the vBNS.

Optical Fibre

An optical fibre is a transparent glass fibre (made of silica or plastic) slightly thicker than a human hair. It functions as a wave-guide, or "light pipe" and is used in optical communications, which permits transmission of data over long distances and at higher band-widths (data-rates, as seen above) than other forms of communication. Instead of metal wires, fibres are used because signals travel along them with little loss and with immunity from electro-magnetic interference. Fibres are also used for illumination,—wrapped in bundles so that they may be used to carry images and to allow viewing in confined spaces. Specially-designed fibres are used for a variety of other applications, including sensors and fibre-lasers.

Basically optical fibres include a transparent core: surrounded by a transparent cladding material with a lower index of refraction. Light is confined to the core by total internal reflection, causing the fibre to act as a wave-guide. Fibres that support many propagation paths or transverse modes are multi-mode fibres (MMF), while those that support only a single mode are single-mode fibres (SMF). MMF generally has wider core diameter and used for short-distance communication links and for applications where higher power is transmitted. SMF is used for communication links longer than 1,050 metres.

India has taken smoothly to fibre optics—the basic science behind the technology—and has a thriving optical fibre industry in both public and private sectors. Examples of MMF is communications through "Intranet" across IGNCA building complex in Delhi, while a multiplex of MMF and SMF prevails for the sea-bed telecommunication links, stretching between south-east Asian countries on one end and the continental Europe at the other end: touching the Indian ports of Chennai and Mumbai in transit.

Joining lengths of optical fibre, incidentally, is more complex than joining electrical wire or cable. The ends of the fibres must be carefully cleaved and then spleened together, either mechanically or by fusing them with heat. Special optical fibre connectors for removable connections are also available.

Web-based Training

On the issue of Indian education, CD-ROMs for computer-based training (CBT) is a comparatively recent phenomenon. Such CDs can be used at home or classroom PCs with massive teaching material. Learning can then be made media-rich in content: mixing text, sound, graphics, animation, simulation and video. The learner can follow his own logical approach and still remain self-paced, depending on individual learning capacity. Learning through CBT, on the other hand, can be organised on a sequential learning path—entirely based on comprehension levels and skills.

Indira Gandhi National Open University (IGNOU) has adopted open distant learning (ODL), in common with other Indian distant learning bodies. In general, ODL is learning at one's own pace: with text and assignments made available by post and learning re-enforced at study-centres with instructors present for problem-solving. ODL in "virtual campus" can emphasis emerging technologies to empower students, using the following IT-based teaching methods:

- Live satellite-based teleconference lectures (accessible at telelearning centres on schedule);
- Recorded video-lectures (as a stand-by to tele-conferencing);
- Practical laboratories (as needed, at distributed study-centres); and
- CBTs (for tutorials).

Internet is made available—at Internet access points—for browsing easily accessible learning resources. Gradually, internet is getting integrated into an instructional design methodology, termed Web-based training (WBT), which also allows for precise tracking of the learning process. WBT identifies the smallest unit of learning and assures its delivery at the topic's end. It is built upon :

1. Attention (held by interacting with graphics and animation);
2. Relevance (with the simulated real-life context);
3. Confidence (derived from reinforcement of learning as above); and
4. Satisfaction (by successful completion and securing high scores in tests).

The instruction design model—followed by the Web-engine—moves from simplicity to complexity using five levels :

- Fact-based content (level1);
- Concept-based content (level 2);
- Application-based content (level 3);
- Analysis-based content (level 4); and
- Synthesis-based content (level 5).

"Collaborative learning" is, in fact, achieved by interaction with peers and content-facilitators—geographically as distributed as Delhi, Dehra Dun, Dubai and Durham—through chat, e-mail, synchronised discussion-forums and posting comments and articles on "blogs".

Convergence

After an uninterrupted reign by huge dinosaurs for millions of years in the Triassic and Jurassic era, it was perhaps the Ice Age in the Cretaceous era that obliterated them. In sharp contrast today, another era has dawned which marks the advent of other "dinosaurs"; technologies like computing, digital signal processing, digital audio-video compression systems, miniaturisation, switching optical fibres and satellite communication. It now appears that these mammoth "dinosaurs" are in for a traumatic change: not for erosion and extinction, but for combination and mutual reinforcement in another Ice Age: of Information (I), Communication (C) and Entertainment (E) !

This has meant *convergence*: of enterprise networks and Internet; of computer, communication, consumer electronics (namely, entertainment); and content industries. The result is an extraordinary union of audio, video and data communication into a *single* source;

received on a *single* device; and delivered by a *single* connection. The process of convergence has made possible the transition from Industrial Age to Information Age; manifest in the new Ice Age.

The consequences are: the use of streaming video transmission over the telecommunication networks, the carriage of voice over computer networks (such as, Internet); and access to Internet through cable on television networks. Consumers themselves are able to create, fit and distribute information as never before! The contemporary visual arts, dance, music, film, theatre and the Web have seen a new coverage. On one end, the convergence process has made possible emergence of global communication networks and satellite networks—leading to a gradual shrinking of geographical borders and distances. At the other end, there is a convergence of the PC with home entertainment system like TV, VCR, and cable TV; and fixed and mobile telephony with Internet.

[A telling commentary on the nature of convergence comes across as the Internet humour: a man of the Ice Age tells his wife, "Darling, the TV is ringing. Will you please attend? I am watching the telephone".]

e-Governance

e-governance is about applying IT in government functions, treating the latter as IT-enabled service. Due to a high dependability on paper in government, digital record-keeping is desirable to meet challenges like the following:

1. Ensuring objectivity in treatment quickly meted out to citizens;
2. Fixing responsibility and enforcing accountability;
3. Creating a durable source of information for future reference; and
4. Using vast data to generate filtered and processed information, for meaningful decision-making.

Thanks to NIC's IT support—planned and implemented at national, State, Union Territory, District and Block development level—there have been major achievements in information analysis; appropriate study; design and development of applications; and necessary training and education. These include:

- District Information System (DISNIC)—Providing decision-support information for economic and social development; programme implementation and project monitoring throughout the country. Over 27 information parameters are identified on structured formats and standard SW packages.
- General Information Service Terminals (GISTNIC)—Providing data on national economy, infrastructure, service-activities, country-profile and IMF/World Bank aids through NICNET terminals at districts, States and Union Territories.
- COURTNIC—Providing the Supreme Court with daily "list of business"; automatic distribution of fresh cases and caveat matching system, followed by case-law information retrieval system (CIRS). This is linked to 18 High Courts in the country where the Supreme Court acts as the gateway on case-status report, lower court-case details, eliminated matters and daily case-list.

These apart, NIC renders support with on-line collection and analysis of country-wide general election results; connectivity to a global medical information system (MEDLARS); industry information linkage to FICCI; and "Information Super-highway" for international sharing of numerous information-sets.

Other notable ventures have included Computerised Rural Information Systems Project (CRISP) in the 1980s and 1990s. Based on the success at Karnataka's Karwar district,, CRISP was extended to: 24 Parganas in West Bengal; Cuttak in Odisha; Hazaribagh in Bihar; Kanpur and Ghaziabad in UP; Betul in MP; Chittoor in AP; Quilon in Kerala; Thane in Maharashtra; Patiala in Punjab; Udaipur in Rajasthan; and Dhubri in Assam.

Pilot projects on land records computerisation have covered Mayurbhanj district in Odisha with great success, besides Singhbhum in Bihar; Morena in MP; Dungarpur in Rajasthan; Ahmedabad in Gujarat; Ranga Reddy in AP; Shonitpur in Assam; and other States afterwards.

The new millennium applications are as follows:

- *AP*—Establishing "Information Kiosks" for citizens paying taxes, collecting birth/death certificates as well a SC/ST certificates, and registering land;

- *Kerala*—Announcing IT policy to make this 100 per cent literate State also an "intelligent State", reducing unemployment and ensuring administration to be citizen-friendly;
- *MP*—Attempting social engineering through IT by running cybercafés-cum- cyber offices ("soochanalaya" or information centre) on low-cost commercial lines, through an intranet network ("gyandoot" or purveyor of knowledge)—to cover development needs of government departments and Panchayats in al 5 blocks of Dhar district.
- *IT Act of 2000*—Going a long way to facilitate e-governance by legal recognition of electronic records and digital signatures, and publication of electronic gazettes.

Outsourcing

"Outsourcing" is a term of comparatively recent origin. Many government departments, business houses and industrial enterprises abroad felt that their IT applications could best be assigned to outside special agencies that could provide those services on contract. India's stakes in outsourcing by Western companies are high. Indian animators are putting in virtual "flesh-and-skeleton" ideas of American film-makers and making these come alive; thanks to the availability of animation SW. Indian engineers are developing complex construction projects abroad,—by single desktop engineering packages. Indian lawyers have embarked on doing legal research for British and American firms. Indian scientists are able to conduct basic and applied R&D for Western firms from their home base.

A new angle has emerged when many First world companies find their back-office workload too massive to be conducted with their expensive manpower and could become cost-effective if passed on to countries like India,—by taking advantage of the networked world. GE-Capital, for instance, has opened in the mid-nineties an international "call centre" at Gurgaon which employs 5,000 people to handle jobs: from answering single queries to collecting money from credit —card users and complex data-mining. Again, e-Funds International of the USA has their back-office operations done at Gurgaon with 2,000 people,—reducing data-processing errors per client by some 90 per cent.

According to the *Economist,* India beckons the USA today for export of the following "IT-enabled" services that grew exponentially to large volumes between the years 2000 and 2005 and continue afterwards:

- Customer interaction centres (e-mail, fax, call services);
- Medical transcription;
- Financial and accounting services;
- Pre-press and digital pre-media;
- Geographic information systems;
- Human resources services;
- Medical billing and collection;
- Distance learning;
- Insurance claims processing; and
- Litigation support services.

The Indian advantages for the above are many and impressive. First, there is a thriving private sector. Second, technology achievements have been remarkable, as evidenced in the cryogenic technology for geo-stationary and polar satellite launching. Third, a high-skilled managerial manpower pool exists. Fourth, there is a robust legal system which could occasionally be a little unwieldy. Finally, there is a comfortable ability to comprehend English language. The earning potentials are overwhelmingly large. Prof. Michael Dentouzos, Director of the MIT Computer Science Laboratory, USA, recently asserted that 50 million English-speaking Indians are capable of annually earning $20,000 per head. This makes a mind-boggling total of $1 trillion,—which is twice India's current GDP !

Technology Incubation

As a part of the ICICI-World Bank funding on technology institution programme, IIT Delhi has begun a Technology Business Incubation Unit (TBIU). Its mission is to promote partnership with new technology entrepreneurs: first-generation, start-up companies and technology-based organisations for a limited period of time for setting up a workstation facility or a prototyping laboratory within the IIT campus. The activities permitted in the TBIU are: product development, product innovation, software testing, simulation, prototyping, pilot experimentation, training and other technology related work on areas like IT in which there exists homology in the institute.

Indians, by turn of the century achieved a remarkable success in Silicon Valley: with 774 companies run by Indian entrepreneurs. Some 300 have each a personal net worth over $5.0 million. They have a collective worth of $25 billion, out of which $6.0 billion are available for reinvestment. On the whole, thrust-areas of growth in the new economic order are: IT and IT-enabled services; bio-technology; energy conservation and alternate technologies; new materials and their applications; and infrastructure (civil, mechanical, telecommunications). India is well-poised to exploit the first three, owing to relatively low resource requirements. India's own strengths in bio-diversity, traditional knowledge of herbs and physiology, and scientific and technical expertise are ideal for the incubation of agricultural, pharmaceutical and health industries.

Among the projects incubated at IIT Delhi, the first fully reversible, male contraceptive is a success in the laboratory and is being scaled up for field trials. IT&T from the USA is supporting IIT to harness intellectual capital and received some 90 proposals for incubation. The projects selected (and provided with mentoring service, seed capital, business-plan structure and infrastructure) are by Datum Technologies (SW services); Hello Pharma (hospital support to the doctor community); and Yatra India (content creation and destination portal). The screening criteria have been homology; good team-potential; clear target to put up an industry; education and academic track-record; and communication potential of ideas.

Customer Relations Management (CRM)

In earlier days, to satisfy an individual customer's demand, the tailor or the craftsman or the retail shopkeeper always strove for "customisation". Later on, "Mass production" saw the setting up of assembly lines, based on general needs of a large number of customers. Now, Levi's and Ford are trying to ascertain the specific need of a customer and dovetail it on-line into the mass production process, to achieve "mass customisation". The secret for the latter is to implement a good amount of enterprise resource planning (ERP) at the back-end: by automating and optimising the internal business areas (Finance, manufacturing, materials, purchase and human relations) and becoming free from the day-to-day business operations. At the front-end, a high-level customer satisfaction is aimed at so that the best customers return for repeat business.

The new focus is to deploy end-to-end systems: customer relations management (CRM) that can deliver personal satisfaction while streamlining the organisation's deployment of resources through ERP. In particular, ERP implementation can result in improving organisation's efficiency, whereas CRM aims at improved effectiveness: by reducing sales cycles and sales costs; identifying new markets and channels of expansion; and improving customer value, satisfaction, retention and overall profitability. Traditional channels of CRM have been personal, face-to-face communications. Availability of electronic technologies of communication have made it possible to reach customers through a variety of channels: call centre; e-mail; SMS in mobiles; direct mail; self-service points; fax; social networking; and field-capture of sales data.

As CRM evolves as a business strategy, customer interaction can be rendered on-line and over multiple channels—including Web channels on the Internet. This allows for the new "e-customer" who can reach the business when and where he wants; place orders at his own terms; use a time convenient to him; and demand prompt and quality service, 24x7. A large number of Indian companies, like Tata Steel, are now deploying "e-CRM" solutions to help business, receive goods; provide after-sales support; add value and track all transactions on the Web. The CRM market itself reached $40 billion by 2004, out of which e-CRM touched $5 billion. It has grown manifold now.

The Siebel Systems is the CRM market leader,—supporting call centre, sales, service and marketing management, in addition to Internet sales and service functions. Major ERP vendors are also adding and integrating CRM applications to their ERP products. Most notable among them are Peoplesoft, SAP and BAAN. Rediff.com is one of the leading Internet portals focussing on the global Indian community. Their solution to establish quality e-customer service network—helped by SMILES CRM package—is that of Carrier Aircon: a leader in air-conditioning equipment.

JAVA

Java's enormous popularity in India (and elsewhere) should be seen for being a programing language for the Internet. It is also an object-oriented language, increasingly important in the world of SW design.

Additionally, it is a cross-platform language that can run on MS Windows, Apple Macintosh and most versions of UNIX operating system. Java extends beyond desk-tops to run on devices like TV, wrist watches and cellular phones. It is, at the same time, quite close to other popular programing languages like C, C++, Pascal and Visual Basics. If one uses Intel-based machine for compilation, the latter does not run on Macintosh, Commodore or other machines. Java, on the contrary, achieves this platform-independence by the use of "virtual machine"—through Java's interim "byte codes".

Stanford University Network (SUN) researchers developed Java—comparable to the Bell Laboratory scientists under AT&T developing the ubiquitous UNIX operating system. The SUN researchers were hoping to develop the language to run the "smart" (microchip-based) appliances of the future: interactive TVs, interactive toasters and interactive lighting for sports tracks, besides a capability of devices to communicate directly with each other. Because it was designed with appliances in mind (rather than PCs), Java had to be *small* (making programs fast to download), *efficient*, *secure* (to prevent hackers from creating havoc) and *portable* ((to run on Windows, Macintosh and other platforms seamlessly.

Java uses object-oriented programing (OOP)—which is a way of conceiving a computer program as a set of interactive objects—and borrows OOP concepts from C++ and other common OOP languages. In addition to its portability and object orientation, Java continues to be smaller and simpler than other comparable languages—stemming from the original need for limited computing muscle and ease to write, compile, debug and run. Although there are several dozen SW packages that can be used to create Java programmes, the most widely used is the Java Development Kit (JDK) from SUN Microsystems: being free of cost and first to circulate.

Java "applets" are small applications that run within a Web-browser. Applets are kept small because they have to be shipped across the network. In a corporate "intranet", where band-width is not an issue, applets could be large. "Servlets", on the contrary, are Java programs that run within a Web-server. They never get transferred to anywhere—catering to fast growth of Java and supporting the following multi-media features:

- In-line sound that plays in real-time whenever a user loads a page;

- Music that plays in the background on a page;
- Cartoon-style animation;
- Real-time video; and
- Multiplier interactive games.

There are many analogous features that have come up with Java. "Java Bean" is the SW component architecture for Java, which allows one to efficiently design applications by configuring and connecting components called "Beans". Microsoft has turned up with Visual J++, to add simple interaction to one's Web-page or write complete stand-alone applications for end-users.

Storage-Area Network (SAN)

As someone put it, in the rush to empower the end-user by decentralizing computer resources, IT managers have lost control over storage. The world-wide web (WWW) has contributed its own share of problems: the Website hits can escalate from thousands to millions and the SW immediately needs to sift data and applications across the enterprise, spread over countries and continents. The answer is now emerging in the form of storage-area network (SAN), getting adopted by leading business houses in India and abroad. SAN is basically a specialised network which is enterprise-wide and allows unfettered exchange of information among hosts and storage devices. The goal is to provide considerable relief in storage, by allowing the end-user have distributed computing power and become "empowered"—without losing control over storage.

The glorious liberation of SAN from, say, LAN or MAN (metropolitan-area network) is achieved through independent fibre channels: as a cross between small computer system interface (SCSI) and Fibrenet. Like SCSI, fibre channels of SAN provide robust connection between storage devices and servers, or clients. Again, like Ethernet (which is a fast LAN up to 100 Mbps developed by XEROX), fibre channels go much beyond the proven technologies of SCSI and Ethernet—by providing extra-fast connectivity—up to 1 Gbps—and spanning 10 km of distance or corporate complex or, when augmented, every 45 km or so. Thus, SAN has a virtually free distribution of space, security and fault-tolerance against potential disasters !

SUN Microsystems announced sometime back in all the Indian Metros that, as data moves to the centre of the new Net Economy, network storage has to fit in: to provide storage solutions to help customers implement mission-critical enterprise-class storage environment. So, seamless scaling of storage resources is happening in India as well !

Portal/Vortal

The mechanism for a portal is straightforward: to develop a working prototype; draw attention (or "eyeballs"); get some venture capital; and then develop one's own portal, regardless of the background: corporations, trades, IT companies, NRIs and professionals like HR, finance, medical or marketing. The most popular portals of the decade that occupy Indian sites in the Internet are: www.indiatimes.com, indiaworld.com, rediff.com, ciol.com, satyamonline.com, indiainfo.com, propertytimes.com, indiainfoline.com, itspace.com, expressindia.com and indiaproperties.com. The following words of caution are necessary :

- Survival is not automatic, in the teeth of competition;
- Portals are not synonymous with a single database and its searching, with contents being of great importance;
- A portal, to be competitive, needs to look at competitors; and
- Media support is vital for the build-up.

In fact, the power of the Internet and the technologies that drive it lie in breaking down large markets of customers into smaller segments and creating a business model: focussed on meeting the needs specific segments. The approach led to developing sites built around niche areas and specific jobs. The brick-and-mortar vertical industry ("vortals") looks—in contrast to portals—for quality customers and value-added transactions in a vertically integrated process.

Someone commented: A vertical portal is about serious business, whereas the horizontal portal is more of fun, frolic and information-mixing with shopping! While horizontal portals spend huge money on promotion and advertising, vortals pump money into conceiving and developing value-added services for focussed audience. To that extent, vortals reflect a mature approach of "narrow-casting" rather than "broadcasting" of horizontal portals—leading to an anticipated upheaval in the latter market.

With the advent of international players in the horizontal portal market, who have deep pockets and innovative strategies and services, a big shake-up is happening. The Internet age has generally shown that—in the world of cut-throat competition—the first portal makes profit, the second averages it out, and the rest continue to make losses or vanish altogether. The history is poised to repeat itself for vortals as well. One way out for horizontal portals is their emerging partnership with vortals. Thus, Satyamonline.com has bought out four of Indiaworld.com's vortals for Rs. 500 crores and are picking stakes in vortals like plasticscommerce.com; cricinfo.com and footforward.com,—the last being o woman-centred portal. Another strategy for horizontal portals is using detailed information and transaction facility on their vertical sectors and promoting themselves as umbrella portals, such as, jaldi.com and indiainfo.com.

Another idea in the dot-com world—snowballing into the Web world—is mobile portal ("mortal"). The wireless application protocol (WAP) as the enabling technology is settling in the market and emerging mortals face a sea-change. Some State governments are moving into WAP for their mobile telephones. It is clear that the days of targeted communication—through a facility like vortal or mortal that can focus on the specific and limited target-audiences—are already here.

Bluetooth

"Deep Blue" and "Bluetooth" both pertain to IT, but the difference between the two is astronomical in proportion. Deep Blue was the hugely powerful IBM supercomputer that stored, *inter alia*, millions of chess-rules: enough to check-mate the Grand Master Kasparov! Bluetooth, on the other hand, is an absolutely tiny microchip, incorporating a radio transceiver built into diverse digital devices. Based upon wireless technology, it is a *de facto* standard with a specification for low cost, short range radio links between mobile PCs, mobile phones and portable electronic devices. The technology resulted from five giants in IT and telecommunication joining in their efforts: Ericsson, Intel, IBM, Nokia and Toshiba. Another 2000 manufacturers—from all parts of the world and various lines of business—also joined the Bluetooth family and in the early 2000's, the technology got embedded into billions of electronic devices.

The Bluetooth wields an enormous capability and makes all connections instantly: without an inch of cable. It facilitates fast and secure transmissions of both voice and data, even when the devices are not within line-of-sight. The radio operates in a globally available frequency-band, ensuring compatibility world-wide. The technology is fully functional even in very noisy radio environment and its voice transmissions are audible under severely trying conditions. The transmission rate is uniformly high and all data are protected by most advanced error-correction methods, incorporating encryption and authentication routines for user-privacy.

The wireless connectivity is like simply switching on the lights. The communication among digital devices remains spontaneous with several advantages. The Bluetooth reality, already in India today, includes the following :

- Mobile phones automatically connect the portable computer to the Internet and operate e-mail;
- Portable computers connect other Bluetooth-enabled devices instantly and automatically,—sending files from one mobile computer to another (as easily as over a LAN) and surfing the Internet regardless of one's location;
- Hand-held devices store all information—calendars, contacts, phone-book, to-do list—and connect wirelessly to any other mobile phone or Bluetooth-enabled wired connection: for e-mails, notes and documents;
- Wireless head-sets offer high sound quality for automatic answering of incoming calls, and initiating voice-activated dial-ups, end-calls, audio-playbacks and volume-control;
- Office equipments can connect wirelessly portable computers (lap-tops) to printers, scanners and faxes,—with wireless mouse and keyboard;
- Cameras, still images and video can send instant "electronic postcard" from any location and transfer still images and video clips between a camera and a portable computer;
- Other electronic devices show virtually unlimited potential,—from hand-held scanners, portable hard disks and wrist watch information centres to refrigerators, coffee machines and presentation projectors;
- Internet access and e-mail are given secure and fast wireless

connection from one's desk-top PCs, mobile computers (lap tops) and hand held devices;
- Office LAN eliminates cable attachments and redefines the meaning of "connective flexibility";
- Wire bound connections operate from any access point within range from one's Bluetooth-enabled device: mobile phone (while on the move) or LAN (while at home or in office), with instant connection.

On the whole, usage-models can be countless: the same phone can switch on to cordless phone (line charge); mobile phone (cellular charge) or walkie-talkie (no telephone charge). The Internet can be surfed and searched wherever one is. The Interactive meetings and conferences can instantly transfer selected documents and exchange electronic business cards. Automatic synchronisation can occur among one's desk-top, lap-top, notebook and mobile phone. Obviously, the prospects are immense !

iPod

Thanks to Steve jobs of Apple Computers, Macintosh from his firm had stunned users with a graphical user interface (GUI) and a mouse as part of computing, way back in 1984. It stirred Nepal, but did not make much headway in India. When Jobs returned to Apple in 1996, he inspired iMac—a computer that blended the monitor with the CPU in one unit. It paved the way for all-in-one devices that are seen in the market today.

In 2001, Jobs produced iPod which was pint-sized and yet at the superior end of portable music players that could store and play music off small hard drives. It could lead music played on tracks for singers to follow. It has, at long last, caught on in India.

Super-computers

In 2005, India was in the fourth position in the world in terms of super-computing capacity. Although super-computing technology was denied to India in the 1990's, our brilliant engineers at C-DAC created PARAM. Even in 2007, India had the world's third largest super-computer. In 2011, just two super-computers from India have made it to the top 500 of the world's best super-computers.

Super-computers are used for highly calculation-intensive tasks, such as, problems involving quantum physics, weather forecasting, climate research, molecular modelling (computing structures and properties of chemical compounds, biological macro-molecules, polymers and crystals), physical simulations (such as, simulation of airplanes in wind tunnels, simulation of the detonation of nuclear weapons).

Other notable frontiers of research where super-computing is used are: in computational fluid dynamics for optimisation of turbines and wings, noise reduction and air-conditioning in trains; in fusion for plasma in a future fusion reactor; in astrophysics for studying the origin and evolution of stars and galaxies; in solid state physics for super-conductivity, surface properties and semi-conductors; in Geophysics for earth quake scenarios; in chemistry for catalytic reactions; in medicine and medical engineering to simulate and control blood-flow, air-conditioning of operations theatres; in biophysics to research on properties of viruses, genome analysis; and in climate research for modelling currents in oceans,— among many other applications.

Japan's 'K Computer' maintains its position atop: capable of performing 10.51 Petaflops/sec on the Linpack benchmark using 705,024 SPARC-64 processing core. At the second place is 'Tianhe-1A' super-computer of the National Super-computing Centre in Tianjin, China, with performance at 2.57 Petaflops/sec.

Cloud Computing

"Cloud" in IT is not something learnt in geography when we were children, but the next frontier for the IT industry to conquer. By 2020, it is expected to be a $650 billion global market and a $16 billion Indian market. The technology visualises a network of servers situated in the Web, which carry out all the processing and storage activities, thus relieving all the need of local computing.

Cloud computing technology enables companies to convert capital expenditure related into operational expenditure, deriving absolute value for money. Through cloud environment, companies can focus on their business and avoid the added cost and complexity of an IT infrastructure and staff without compromising on business deliverables. Cloud computing is an excellent example of technology that fits this requirement. Small businesses and mid-size companies need to ensure growth while conducting business in a smart, lean and cost-effective way. This means streamlining customer-facing business processes while scaling them across organisational and international boundaries.

Cloud technology helps small businesses by providing the functional depth of a large-scale business management solution. Indians typically are not privy to compliance and regulatory issues. Many companies are adopting cloud solution as a subsidiary enterprise resource planning (ERP) system. The powerful solution meets functional and industry requirements, provides deep integration with ERP used at headquarters and is easily deployable, simpler to manage and easier to change. The cloud platform suitably fits into this milieu by enabling information exchange to be imbibed in the business environment in a simpler, more affordable way. The application connects customers and suppliers for business-to-business e-commerce. It helps establish a connection with a business partner once for each process and instantly exchange related electronic documents, such as, purchase orders, forecasts, invoices, and delivery notes, using your existing applications.

Can someone we do not know build a plug-in for our sales lead rating that is built to connect with our cloud CRM? Is there a template for the chemical industry that can be downloaded for our cloud ERP? Cloud solutions are modified to enable "processes outsourcing" by driving sustainable cost savings, comprehensive contract management, to provide superior supplier management, and to help ensure rapid time to value. Sales professionals in India, who are perpetually on the go—covering huge Indian topography and beating the traffic and congestion—can now collaborate on business opportunities through cloud based CRM. Such cloud application helps them with real time information updates, and a new user experience. One can concentrate on one's business goals. It is small—simple—easy but has a high ROI for companies with fat travel bills.

With growth and industrialisation, India is increasingly becoming susceptible to environmental impacts. Our carbon emission is expected to rise to an alarming 3.5 tonnes by 2030 (Source: *Economic Survey* 2009 - 2010). It is the responsibility of corporate India to safeguard the future of its next generations. Governments have slowly and steadily started laying rules for environmental compliance. It is critical for a global organisation to accurately measure, mitigate, and monitor green-house gas emissions and other environmental impacts, such as, solid waste and water. In the cloud, there are applications that can cost-effectively assess one's total carbon emissions inventory across all scopes, provide transparency into one's sustainability initiatives, establish a comprehensive inventory of carbon emissions and achieve cost savings by identifying opportunities for energy, waste, and emissions reductions within and outside operational boundaries. Becoming a green enterprise is the only sustainable direction for a company if it wants to succeed. And collectively, that is the way forward for India, Inc.

India is, therefore, uniquely suited to really take advantage of cloud computing to achieve its goals for the future. While China has always played the volume game, it left Europe and America to play the value game. We firmly believe that with the power of the cloud, India can get really good value for volume and we will see an exponential growth in the creation and consumption of cloud applications.

Nanotechnology

Nanotechnology deals with a billionth of a metre. It handles vast amounts of data—by rearranging atoms—to structure molecules and create new materials. For instance, the repair of a diseased tissue needs a very precise process and one needs a nano-level robot to restore the tissue. The same applies for removal of capillary obstruction in one's body.

It is today regarded as a revolutionary technology that can help address key needs relating to energy, environment, health and agriculture in developing countries as follows:

- Nanotechnology development in the fore-runner countries is characterised by, *inter alia*, increased investment in research and development (R&D), development of competitive R&D infrastructure, inter-disciplinary education and training system together with development of entrepreneurship, technology transfer and innovation and contribution to economic growth.
- Reconfiguration of existing institutional structures and evolution of new forms of collaborative arrangements between various actors and policies has emerged as an important factor enabling these countries to remain fore-runner in nanotechnology.
- The R&D focus in nanotechnology globally is diverse with countries developing technologies in areas corresponding to

their own expertise and needs. There is a need for development of clear national strategies to utilise nanotechnology to meet social priorities.

- A deliberate innovation policy in nanotechnology, with the government acting as a guide in areas where market signals are weak and are not sufficient on their own, is important for alignment of nanotechnology with overall societal goals.
- To engage with nanotechnology successfully, developing countries would need to address a range of issues pertaining to research, technology development, skills requirement, institutions involved, risks issues, regulatory and governance structure and stakeholder engagement.
- Nanotechnology development in India is at a nascent stage with policy initiatives directed towards promoting research and development. It is largely a government-led initiative and industry participation is still emerging. A more inclusive science and technology (S&T) policy-making process and integrated framework is needed to ensure that this technology is diffused and used for socially valued goods.
- The likelihood of adverse impacts to environment and human health as well as consumer and worker safety exists along the life cycle of nano-applications. Given the variety of nano-materials and their broad-spectrum applications, the nature of hazards from these substances might be varied and even unforeseen. However, risks from nanotechnology-based materials and products would depend on the nature of impacts and the degree, stage and duration of exposures.
- An inclusive and responsive risk-governance structure to address multi-dimensional risks from nanotechnology is imperative. There is a need to put in place adequate structures to carry out risk-assessment procedures and ensure laws and policies that would address the liability and redress issues inherent in the application of nanotechnology: having unknown environmental and health impacts.
- Regulatory oversight for nanotechnology is necessary to channelise research efforts in a responsible direction. The regulatory regime for nanotechnology needs to be dynamic and should be reviewed from time to time. Transparency and public involvement in the design and implementation of regulatory structure in nanotechnology should be ensured.

National Foundation of Indian Engineers conducted a study in 2008 which made the following important observations:

1. Nanotechnology has great opportunities, not only for science and research but also for industrial production and usage in everyday life of individuals;
2. The rapid development of nanotechnology is often considered as a fundamental revolution in technology as compared with the discovery of antibiotics, drug delivery, biotechnology, health care, materials and metallurgy, electronics, etc.;
3. With the emerging focus on nanotechnology, an increasing demand for qualified manpower will arise in the next few years in industrial fields, such as, production, quality assurance, etc.;
4. Skill-gaps in the nano-field may occur if education and training systems do not react in time. This may significantly diminish its growth potential and employment both in academia and industry;
5. In the academia, publications provide only an analytical overview. Product development is, however, lacking;
6. In the Industry side, experts are interested in the commercialisation of the R&D work. R&D work is mostly in preliminary stages, particularly in drug and pharmaceutical sector.
7. Since nanotechnology is a new area, few quality standards exist so far.
8. Institutions for education and training centres of excellence, exclusively in the area of nanotechnology, need be more strongly promoted by the Government;
9. Funding should be focussed and needs be done for more institutes who come forward for application-oriented R&D projects;
10. Networking between inter-institutes and inter-departments is minimal. Similarly, networking and resource-sharing between R&D labs and Industry is also low.

Global Positioning System (GPS)

The Global Positioning System (GPS) is a satellite-based navigation system made up of a full constellation of 24 satellites, placed into orbit by the USA. In the 1980s, the US Government made the system available for civilian use. GPS works in any weather conditions, anywhere in the world, 24 hours a day. There are no subscription fees or set-up charges to use GPS. GPS satellites circle the earth twice a day in a very precise orbit and transmit signal information to earth. GPS receivers take the information and use triangulation to calculate the user's exact location. Essentially, the GPS receiver compares the time a signal was transmitted by a satellite with the time it is received. The time-difference tells the GPS receiver how far away the satellite is. Now, with distance measurements from a few more satellites, the receiver can determine the user's position and display it on the unit's electronic map.

A GPS receiver must be locked on to the signal of at least three satellites to calculate a 2-D position (latitude and longitude) and track movement. With four or more satellite in view, the receiver can determine the user's 3-D position (latitude, longitude and altitude). Once the user's position has been determined, the GPS unit can calculate other informations, such as, speed, bearing, track, trip distance, distance to destination, sunrise and sunset time and more. Today's GPS receivers are extremely accurate, thanks to their parallel multi-channel design. Gramin's 12 parallel-channel receivers are quick to lock onto satellites when first turned on and they maintain strong locks, even in dense foliage or urban settings with tall buildings. Certain atmosphere factors and other sources of error can affect the accuracy of GPS receivers. Gramin GPS receivers are accurate to within 15 metres on average.

Number of satellites visible is a factor; with more satellites a GPS receiver can 'see' providing better accuracy. Buildings, terrains, electronic interferences or sometimes even dense foliages can block signal reception, causing position errors or possibly no position-reading at all. GPS units typically would not work indoors, underwater or underground.

In India, GPS has become vastly popular by being incorporated in mobile phones. GPS is also independently available for being attached to moving cars which is done in all Metro cities.

Google's Transliteration Effort

The latest to contribute to the development of SW offering uniform platform to Indian languages is the software giant Google. Transliteration is the method to enable users to enter text in one of the supported languages using a Roman keyboard. Users can type a word the way it sounds using Latin characters and transliteration script will convert the word to its native script. Till recently this service was offered online only—meaning that you need an internet connection for transliteration. Now Google has launched the new transliteration SW—"Google Transliteration IME" which enables offline transliteration as well. This is available today for 14 different Indian languages—Arabic, Bengali, Farsi (Persian), Greek, Gujarati, Hindi, Kannada, Malayalam, Marathi, Nepali, Punjabi, Tamil, Telugu and Urdu.

K-Yan : The Compact Media Centre

New-generation communication technologies allow creation of novel media products that can serve the community at large. Such products must be robust, and possess simple and universal interfaces. Prof. Kirti Trivedi of IDC has developed "K-Yan", a compact media product for community use. It combines the functions of a multi-media and Internet-enabled PC, large format television, DVD/VCD/CD player, CD writer, video-conference device, LCD data projector, and an audio system that facilitates shared viewing and participation by users. Launched in March 2004, K-Yan has been demonstrated to several Chief Ministers, and senior State and Central government officials. K-Yan is easy to use, has multilingual facilities, and eliminates the need for investing in other media hardware. A single unit can cater to the teaching needs of an entire class, and substantially reduce the cost of computerising schools.

The integration of various functions not only allows students to learn how to use a computer, but also other subjects, and crafts. The product will also be useful in other group learning or information dissemination programs like healthcare, family planning, agricultural practices, and civic awareness drives. K-Yan is equipped with extra solar energy-based portable power supply to enable use in areas with no electricity. Mounted on a van, it can also function as a mobile communication centre from remote locations. With an Internet connection and a web-camera, it would allow low cost web-conferencing from any location making it useful in disaster management or project progress monitoring. The web-conferencing feature will also be useful in e-governance, as it will facilitate direct communication between various agencies and the administration.

K-Yan has evoked enthusiastic response and is on the way to becoming a major commercial success.

An Indian's 'Sixth Sense'

A 28-year-old Indian doctoral student at MIT, Pranav Mistry, has developed a revolutionary technology called 'Sixth Sense'. His invention of 'Sixth Sense / WUW (Wear UR World)' is a wearable gestural, user-friendly interface linking the physical world around us with digital information and using hand gestures to interact with them. The device sees what we see but it lets out information that we want to know while viewing the object. It can project information on any surface, be it a wall, table or any other object and uses hand / arm movements to help us interact with the projected information. The device brings us closer to reality and assists us in making right decisions by providing the relevant information, thereby making the entire world a computer. Still more work needs to be done on the device and, when fully developed, it will revolutionise the world.

Tablet Computers

Finally, the following list takes a look at the various "tablets"—both local and foreign-made—that are available in the Indian market. They pander to varying budgets and requirements, as may be expected, with approximate prices given below:

Apple iPad2

Operating System	: IOS
Screen	: 10" (capacitive)
Network	: 3G and wi-fi
Processor	: 1 GHz
RAM	: 246 MB
Memory	: 16 GB
Camera	: Yes
Price	: Rs. 32,000

Aakash Tablet

Operating System	: Android 2.2

Screen	: 7” (reflective)
Network	: 3G and wi-fi
Processor	: 366 MHz
RAM	: 256 MB
Camera	: External USB
Price	: Rs. 2,999 (concessional for students)

Beetle Magiq

Operating System	: Android 2.3
Screen	: 7" (capacitive)
Network	: 3G and wi-fi
Processor	: 1 GHz
RAM	: 256 MB
Memory	: 8 GB
Camera	: Yes
Price	: Rs. 9,999

Blackberry Playbook

Operating System	: Blackberry OS
Screen	: 7" (capacitive)
Network	: 3G and wi-fi
Processor	: 1 GHz
RAM	: 1 GB
Memory	: 16 GB
Camera	: Yes
Price	: Rs. 27,990

Reliance 3G Tab

Operating System	: Android 2.3
Screen	: 7" (capacitive)
Network	: 3G and wi-fi
Processor	: 800 MHz
RAM	: 512 MB
Memory	: 4 GB
Camera	: Yes
Price	: Rs. 12,999

Samsung Galaxy

Operating System	: Android 2.2
Screen	: 10" (capacitive)
Network	: 3G and wi-fi
Processor	: 500 MHz
RAM	: 1 GB
Memory	: 32 GB
Camera	: Yes
Price	: 29,299

× × ×

Coming to my conclusion, IT has moved a long way from where I had begun: groping with the nascent Management Studies' graduate degree under BIM, UK in 1966: moving into computers in Manchester and, later, on both sides of the Atlantic in the defence domain where computers had grown first, as "Commonwealth Scholar" in 1968-72; negotiating with UNDP who took a dim view of India's capacity to use computers in 1974; Meeting industry, business and education stalwarts at the ASCI Court of Governors who had an equally biased notion against computers in India in 1978-80; and the country-wide severe Leftist prejudice against computers—"killing' employment, if allowed in India!—in Rajiv Gandhi's regime in the entire 1980-90 that we had passed through. Obviously, Mohammed—the common man—had not gone to the proverbial Mountain—the cold, distant and unfriendly computer—as yet.

Since then the tables have turned and, if anything, Mountain has most definitely come to Mohammed,—with computer coming down into everyday life of man, its inventor, in the most intimate of terms imaginable. IT has become a part and parcel of our daily lives, and its uses are almost beyond comprehension itself. The present-day computers are used to work, to play, to have fun, to shop, to study, to talk, to date and to generally do anything one can think about. Computers have replaced human beings in so many fields that it is easy to list those tasks where it has failed to replace humans till date. Thankfully, computers cannot replace humans in those fields where feelings, taste, experience, judgment and creativity are required. However, efforts are on to add these attributes as well to computer.

Let us take a look at some of the familiar uses of computer today:

Word Processing—Word Processing SW automatically corrects spelling and grammatical mistakes. If the content of a document repeats, one does not have to type it each time. One can use the copy-and-paste features. One can print documents and make several copies. It is easier to read a word-processed document than a hand-written one. One can add images to one's document. Storing names and addresses in an address book or making a list of the books that one owns can be called information management. SW can be used to store contact information, generating plans, scheduling appointments and deadlines.

Modelling—When a computer is used to design a logo or create a spreadsheet to work out the cost of something, it is being used for "modelling". Just as we might make a model of a house to see what it will look like when it is built, so with a computer, we can create a model to try things out. Even writing with a word processor can sometimes be called modelling if we are changing words to try to improve our writing. Different types of certificates can be generated. It is very easy to create and change layouts. With desktop publishing, one can create page layouts for entire books on personal computer.

Leisure—Sometimes we may use a computer just for fun. Some computers, often called "games consoles" are actually specially designed for playing games.

Mathematical Calculations—Thanks to computers, which have computing speeds of over a million calculations per second, we can perform the biggest of mathematical calculations in any work situation or scientific experiment.

Business—The owner of a small business might use a computer to help them manage their business. Even businesses use computers in different ways. For example, the owner of a shop may use a computer to: record how many of each item they sell; work out how much to charge a customer; keep track of the number of each item they have on their shelves; order new stock; design and print displays and prices; and many other uses.

Internet—It is an invisible network of almost all the computers in the world. One can browse through much more information than one does in a library. One also has very fast and convenient access to information. Through e-mail, one can communicate with a person sitting thousands of miles away in a few seconds. In social networking,

"Chat" software enables one to chat with another on a real-time basis. Video-conferencing tools are becoming readily available to the common man. Even designing a picture-poster to advertise something may be communicating. One can also see results of any examination on the Internet. There are many alumni websites through which one can regain contact with one's classmates. One can send and receive e-greetings cards pertaining to different occasions.

e-commerce—This is a general term describing buying or selling things using a computer. If students or their families have ever bought something over the Internet, they have been using e-commerce.

Digital Video or Audio Composition—Audio or video composition and editing have been made much easier by computers. It no longer costs thousands of dollars of equipment to compose music or make a film. Graphics engineers can use computers to generate short or full length films or even to create 3D models. Anybody owning a computer can now enter the field of media production. Special effects in science fiction and action movies are created using computers.

Medicine—Computer software is used for diagnosis of diseases and for examination of internal organs of the body. Advanced computer based systems are used to examine organs of the body. Some of the complex surgeries can be performed with the help of computers. Computer-assisted Surgery (CAS) is a fast advancing field in medicine, which combines medical expertise with computer intelligence to give faster and more accurate results in surgical procedures. Computers are excellent means for storage of patient-related data. Hospitals employ computer systems to maintain patient records. Doctors use computers to store information about a patient's family history, physical ailments in the family (if any), already diagnosed diseases and prescribed medicines. Computers can keep track of prescriptions and billing information. They can be used to store information about the medicines prescribed to a patient as well as those, which cannot be prescribed (ones which the patient is allergic to).

Hospitals—Different types of monitoring equipment in hospitals are often based on computer programing. Many modern methods of scanning and imaging are largely based on computer technology. Sophisticated computers and infra-red cameras are used for obtaining high-resolution images. The functioning of hospital bed beeping systems, emergency alarm systems, X-ray machines and several such medical appliances are based on computer logic. Today, it is possible to obtain experts' opinions within seconds by means of the Internet. Medical practitioners can discuss medical issues in medical forums.

Banks—All financial transactions can be done by IT, like Electronic Cash Service (ECS) for payment of telephone bills, credit cards, electricity bills, etc. They provide security, speed and convenience, and avoid drudgery. The computer SW authenticates the user and dispenses cash by ATM machine.

Travel—One can book air tickets or Railway tickets and make hotel reservations on-line far ahead of one's travel schedule—sitting at the comfort of home. The owner of a travel agent might use their computers for similar tasks but probably make more use of the computer as a way of finding information, such as, flight times or hotel vacancies as well as using it much more to communicate with customers and suppliers such as hotels and airlines.

Telecommunications—SW is widely used here. Also all mobile phones—which have widely spread today—have software embedded in them.

Defence—There is software embedded in almost every weapon. SW is used for controlling the flight and targeting in ballistic missiles. SW is used to control access to atomic bombs.

e-Learning—Instead of a book it is easier to learn from an e-learning SW.

Retail Trade—Shops and supermarkets use SW, which calculate the bills. Taxes can be calculated and paid on-line. Accounting is done using computers. One can predict future trends of business using artificial intelligence SW. SW is used in major stock markets. There are fully or partially automated factories running on SW.

Car—Some parts of cars are made by computer-controlled machines. Computers are even used to manage the robots that assemble the parts of the car in many car-assembly factories.

Marriage—There are matrimonial sites through which one can use to search for a suitable groom or bride.

News—There are many Websites through which one can read the latest or old news, such as, the Sunday magazine-supplements of a daily paper from anywhere.

Robotics—Robots, in business or in games, are controlled by SW.

Electronic Gadgets—They run with the help of computers. There are various SW products which are used to increase the efficiency of these devices. Timers, self-controlled switches: all these ensure that the machines ask for minimum human effort. A computer may be used to control a microwave oven in order to prepare food so computers are used to control machines which make the parts used in making products.

Sports—SW is used for making umpiring decisions. There is simulation SW used which a sportsperson can practice his skills. Computers are also to identify flaws in technique.

Airplanes—Pilots train on software, which simulates flying. Planes are generally flown by computer—called "auto-pilot"—for most of their journey and, at many airports it is a computer that lands the plane, not the pilot.

Weather Analysis—Super-computers are used to analyse and predict weather. India is high on the global list of countries with the most powerful super-computers. Facilities like super-computers are for the disposal of elite intellectuals like scientists, engineers and policy makers and makes indirect impact on the population in general.

× × ×

Indian society, in general, has awakened to IT revolution and technological advances are also being made taking into consideration the requirement of different segments of the society. For a country with large population and scarce resources, computer technology comes as a great tool for social transformation. It has already revolutionised the field of communication and in convergence with mobile and internet technology is changing the way India communicates as follows:

Agriculture—Technological advances have brought about drastic changes in farming and animal husbandry in the West resulting in tremendous increase in production capacity. The most common use of computers has been in replacing human effort and intervention in traditional farming machinery and other equipment. If computers have changed the ways of farming, then the Internet has only doubled that pace of change. Geographic Information Systems (GIS) are being used for developing ranking systems that evaluate land. These hi-tech, interactive systems provide information based on a variety of factors such as soil conditions, drainage and slope conditions, soil pH and nutrient status, etc.

Telephone—When we telephone someone, not only do computers make sure we are connected to the right telephone number, but they also keep track of how much time we spend talking so that our telephone bill is accurate and up-to-date.

Television and Radio—Television and radio not only use computers to manage their broadcasts they also use them to create the programmes in the first place. Modern television cameras have computers within them and the editing of the video they collect is done by people using computers just like we might use a computer to create and edit our writing using a word processor.

Satellites—It is computers that manage the satellites themselves and keeps them in position,—providing in formation on imminent cyclones to ships, airlines, farmers marketing their agro-products in distant markets and intrepid fishermen venturing into high seas for days together, as well as forecast schools of fish in certain marine zones to the latter.

Automatic Control—Automatic computer-controlled processes are used to control traffic lights and lifts in tall buildings. Television, radio, telephones and the Internet are all managed and controlled automatically by computers.

On-line—One can give on-line examinations and get instant results. One can check one's examination results on-line. One can also apply for a job or admission in a school or a college by filling the application form on-line. This saves time and energy. Tax returns can also be filed on the Internet. Income Tax form can be downloaded from the Income tax website. One can even gamble on-line instead of going to a casino. One can do trading on-line.

Legal-Help —Computer application is also being extended to legal arena. The Supreme Court of India has become the first court in the country to provide e-filing of cases.

× × ×

Education—Thanks to computers, imparting education has become easier and much more interesting than before. Owing to memory capacities of computers, large chunks of data can be stored in them. They enable quick processing of data with very less or no chances of errors in processing. Networked computers aid quick communication and enable Web-access. Storing documents or computers in the form of soft copies instead of hard ones helps save paper. The advantages of computers in education primarily include :

1. Storage of information;
2. Quick data processing;
3. Audio-visual aids in teaching;
4. Better presentation of information;
5. Access to the Internet; and
6. Quick communication between students, teachers and parents.

IT has made the dream of distance learning, a reality. Education is no longer limited to classrooms. Physically distant locations have come closer due to Internet accessibility. There are many online educational courses, whereby students are not required to attend classes or be physically present for lectures. IT has given impetus to distance education. Computers facilitate effective presentation of information. Presentation software like PowerPoint and animation software like Flash among others can be of great help to teachers while delivering lectures. Computers facilitate audio-visual presentation of information, thus making the process of learning interactive and interesting. Computer-aided teaching adds a fun element to education. Due to the visual aid, difficult subjects can be explained in better ways. Things become easier to follow, thanks to the use of computers in education. Computer software can help better presentation of information.

Both teachers and students benefit from the Internet. Teachers can refer to it for additional information and references on the topics to be taught. Students can refer to web sources for additional information on subjects of their interest. The Internet helps teachers set test papers, frame questions for home assignments and decide project topics. And not just academics, teachers can use Web sources for ideas on sports competitions, extracurricular activities, and more. Computers enable access to the Internet which has information on literally everything. Computers enable storage of data in the electronic format, thereby saving paper. Memory capacities of computer storage devices are in gigabytes. This enables them to store huge chunks of data. The process becomes paperless.

Computers have become the life-line of young generation. The present generation students like to embrace all the things in the ambit of this modern technology. The educators are feeling shy and reluctant to accept technology as their work partner. Will our present and the immediate next generation educators like to view the gap widening between them and further generation students in terms of usage of technology for teaching learning purpose, or, they would like to modernise themselves in the struggle to keep intact their responsible professional position intact? Are universities and institutions in the field of teacher education focussing upon the courses for using computers in education, or, they simply feel delighted to see the State boards at school level and National/State councils for Educational Research and Training (NCERT/SERT) advancing at great speed to plan out integration of technology with education,—with teachers struggling to complete even the prescribed syllabus ?

In order to meet the challenges provided by present society, many universities in the field of teacher education had introduced an optional course in computers. This only brought awareness about computers in the field of teacher education. The student-teachers were made to know about basic computer hardware and some software application packages. NCERT has urged to focus upon integration of technology with education, yet many universities have not reframed their traditional curriculum for Teacher Education. And those universities who tried to initiate the process were faced by different challenges including lack of specialists and professionals to frame proper curriculum, curriculum as per needs of modern developing India with global economy, teacher educators and study material for such curriculum, etc. There are indeed many specialised teachers and a plethora of study material for technical knowledge in computers, but we lack teacher educators and resources for teaching computers in education.

e-tutor can give access to teachers instantly and give a better chance to earn. Current syllabus can be viewed through website of the concerned school board; made available to students if teacher has made a website and uploaded using Internet; and updating, using web could be done easily. e-books, on-line libraries and on-line encyclopedias help to guide in minutes and save precious time and resources. Other current and potential applications are:

- Keeping records of students for their academic scores;
- Keeping records in relation to personal history;
- Creating question bank for students;
- Using computers for testing by asking questions from question bank;
- Online Testing and Evaluation;

- Analysis and interpretation of the data; and
- Previous year question Papers and sample papers using web sites.

Library—Documents stored as soft copy for students/faculty members can use on-line magazines, journals, brochures, research articles; records of the books are maintained using special library SW. Records of the issues and returns of the books are maintained on-line.

School Administration—These can include records of students (personal, academic, financial); records of employees of school; accounts of the institution; aid to memory with minimum paper work; current regulations of government and affiliating school boards and related authorities; fees collection and maintenance of fees record; circulation of instruction/notices and getting it in printed form; preparation of school magazine.

Rather than kill employment, computerisation has created a lot of jobs, such as, DTP operators, Programers, HW and SW professionals. It provides tremendous openings for new kinds of entrepreneurs and gives employment opportunity for women (including housewives) to work from home on part-time basis.

The computer also has its negative side. The rise of cyber crime, the use of chat rooms for indecent discussion, certain Websites dealing in pornographic material, etc., have been noticed. But the advantages and importance outweigh the disadvantages. Through computerisation, the world has become a global village today.

Bibliography

Athalye, Neeraj, "Cloud Computing Embodies the Essence of India", Working Paper, date unspecified.

Banerjee, Utpal K. and Sachdeva, R.K., *Management Information System: A New Framework,* Vikas Publishing House, New Delhi, 1995.

Banerjee, Utpal K., "Control Informatics—Its Role in Developing Countries" and "Appropriate Informatics in Industry: A Third World Viewpoint", two papers in FG Foster, Ed., *Informatics and Industrial Development,* Tycooly International Publishing, Dublin, 1982.

Banerjee, Utpal K., "Country Report: India", paper in Saito, Prof Tadao, Ed., *Information Technology-led Development: A Report of APO Basic Research on IT,* Asian Productivity Organisation, Tokyo, 1990.

Banerjee, Utpal K., "Electronic Media for Cultural Education", paper in Srivastava, S.L., Ed., *Electronics for Teaching and Mass Education—Proceedings of the National Seminar,* National Academy of Sciences, Allahabad, 1986.

Banerjee, Utpal K., "Operational Research and Government of India", paper in Brans, J.P., Ed., *Operational Research 81—Ninth IFORS International Conference on Operational Research,* North-Holland, Amsterdam, 1981.

Banerjee, Utpal K., "User Education in Informatics and Its Impact", paper in Barta, B.Z. and Raab, B.B. Ed., *The Impact of Informatics on Vocational and Continuing Education,* North-Holland, Amsterdam, 1985

Banerjee, Utpal K., *Common Man's Guide to Computers: Concepts, Applications, Issues,* Concept Publishing Co., New Delhi, 1992.

Banerjee, Utpal K., *Computer Management and Planning,* Tata McGraw-Hill Publishing Co, New Delhi, 1987.

Banerjee, Utpal K., *Computer! Computer!—A Science Play for Children,* Madhubani Education Books, Vikas Publishing House, New Delhi, 1986.

Banerjee, Utpal K., Ed., *Computer Application for Rural Development,* Vikas Publishing House, New Delhi, 1987.

Banerjee, Utpal K., Ed., *Computer Applications for techno-Economic Development,* Concept Publishing Co., New Delhi, 1985.

Banerjee, Utpal K., Ed., *Computer Education in India: Past,, Present and Future,* Published for IETE, Concept Publishing Co., New Delhi, 1996.

Banerjee, Utpal K., Ed., *Information Technology for Common Man,* Concept Publishing Co., New Delhi, 1992.

Banerjee, Utpal K., *Information Management in Government,* Concept Publishing Co., New Delhi, 1984.

Banerjee, Utpal K., *Management Perspectives,* AIMA-VIKAS Management Series, Vani Educational Books, New Delhi, 1984.

Banerjee, Utpal K., *Management Strategy for Information Technology: IT and Management Convergence,* Concept Publishing Co, New Delhi, 2008.

Banerjee, Utapal K., *Operational Analysis and Indian Defence,* Concept Publishing Co., New Delhi, 1980.

Banerjee, Utpal K., *Practical Management Information System: Indian Experiences and Case Studies,* Macmillan India, New Delhi, 2001.

Computer Division, ASCI, *Management Game: With Computer Aid,* Administrative Staff College of India, Hyderabad, 1978.

National Foundation of Indian Engineers, *Study on Status of Nanotechnology in Indian Industry and Academia /R&D Labs,* Department of Science & Technology, GoI, National Science & Technology Management Information System (NSTMIS), New Delhi, 2008.

Rao, S.L., *From Servants to Masters?: The Evolution of Professional Management in India,* Global Business Series, All India Management Association, New Delhi, 2007.

Sharma, Dinesh C., *The Long Revolution: The Birth and Growth of India's IT Industry,* Harper Collins India, New Delhi, 2009.

The Energy and Resource Institute (www.teriin.org) +, *Nanotechnology Development in India: The Need to Building Capability and Governing the Technology,* Briefing Paper, TERI, New Delhi, 2010.

× × ×

Index